Creative Ide
Frontline Evangelism
with Young People

Simon Rundell

CANTERBURY
PRESS
Norwich

© Simon Rundell 2013

Published in 2013 by Canterbury Press
Editorial office
3rd Floor
Invicta House
108–114 Golden Lane
London
EC1Y 0TG

Canterbury Press is an imprint of Hymns Ancient & Modern Ltd
(a registered charity)
13A Hellesdon Park Road
Norwich NR6 5DR, UK

www.canterburypress.co.uk

British Library Cataloguing in Publication data

A catalogue record for this book is available
from the British Library

978 1 84825 276 9

Typeset by Regent Typesetting, London
Printed and bound by
CPI Group (UK) Ltd, Croydon

Contents

Introduction

My first two adventures in print (*Creative Ideas for Alternative Sacramental Worship* and *Creative Ideas for Sacramental Worship with Children*)[1] were primarily concerned with a missional approach using the sacraments: creative methods to enable people to sense Christ's presence in the world and in their own lives. It was overwhelmingly a multi-sensual approach intended to draw the soul into an engagement with the divine. Through my work with the Blessed Community and many years of youth ministry, we have attempted to reach out to the sacred through ritual and through the essential stories which tell of the Christian faith.

One of the things that has become most apparent in my priestly work with young people is how little of the cultural baggage of Christianity the young now possess: how the signs, symbols and most significantly the stories of the Bible and the Church have become lost to them. One could see this as a result of the postmodern age, as multiple narratives and sources of authority have crowded into our lives; as religious diversity has influenced our previous monoculture (which I believe to be a good thing) and as some aspects of the conservative agenda of faith threaten to change Christianity into a monster which harangues and bullies rather than loves and serves.

Rather than bewail this or see it as a portent of the demise of the Church, we should see it as an opportunity for fresh evangelism on a blank canvas. The opportunity is presented because the stories of Christ and the early Church are so alive, so captivating and dynamic that they cannot fail to engage new audiences, hungry for timeless stories and the eternal truths that God reveals through them.

---

1 S. Rundell, *Creative Ideas for Alternative Sacramental Worship*, Canterbury Press, 2010; S. Rundell, *Creative Ideas for Sacramental Worship with Children*, Canterbury Press, 2011.

The genesis of this book is in practical and down-to-earth youth work, rather than dry and removed academic research. In the presence of teenagers with no previous engagement with faith and having tried and failed with a few other approaches and techniques,[2] I exasperatedly retold them a Bible story in a modern context, from the perspective of one who was there, taking the events from the page and putting them into the mouth of a witness. The story was that of Jesus walking on the water.[3] For once, these 40 restless and usually noisy, unengaged young people were still, drawn into the story, eager to hear the outcome and most importantly the message behind it. 'It was just like in that *Bruce Almighty* film, Farv!' one of them exclaimed after I had half-acted my part as Peter, jumping over the side and then starting to sink when I thought I could manage the miracle on my own, only to be rescued by Christ reaching out to me. The original Bible illustration was new to them, the point of reference a well-loved film.

It was a turning point in our ministry to those young people, as we realized that they lacked the cultural language which so many within the Church possess. The Church takes for granted its own heritage and has lost its missionary zeal in the telling and retelling of these stories. Subsequently these retellings have been refined and reinterpreted for the context of young people, especially those who are on the peripheries of faith.

The Purpose of this Book

It is in the context of young people that this book is called *Frontline Evangelism with Young People*, recognizing that often in youth clubs, schools, Sunday schools and other youth work settings we are increasingly encountering young people who know nothing of Christ. This is the frontline of mission and the place to which Christ calls us to make his name known. Vincent Donovan writes of his work with the Maasai tribe in Africa[4] and yet when I re-read it, he could so easily be speaking of working with tribes of young people. Standing in front of a (seemingly) intimidating group of teenagers reminds me of Paul venturing into the Areopagus in Acts 17:

---

2 Including some of my better and more imaginative alternative worship ideas – living proof that what works for some will not necessarily work with others.

3 Matthew 14.22–33.

4 V. Donovan, *Christianity Rediscovered*, SCM Press, 2001.

Then the Epicurean and Stoic philosophers took him and brought him to a meeting of the Areopagus, where they said to him, 'May we know what this new teaching is that you are presenting? You are bringing some strange ideas to our ears, and we would like to know what they mean.' (All the Athenians and the foreigners who lived there spent their time doing nothing but talking about and listening to the latest ideas.) Paul then stood up in the meeting of the Areopagus and said: 'People of Athens! I see that in every way you are very religious. For as I walked around and looked carefully at your objects of worship, I even found an altar with this inscription: "TO AN UNKNOWN GOD". So you are ignorant of the very thing you worship – and this is what I am going to proclaim to you.

'The God who made the world and everything in it is the Lord of heaven and earth and does not live in temples built by human hands. And he is not served by human hands, as if he needed anything. Rather, he himself gives everyone life and breath and everything else. From one man he made all the nations, that they should inhabit the whole earth; and he marked out their appointed times in history and the boundaries of their lands. God did this so that they would seek him and perhaps reach out for him and find him, though he is not far from any one of us. "For in him we live and move and have our being." As some of your own poets have said, "We are his offspring."

'Therefore since we are God's offspring, we should not think that the divine being is like gold or silver or stone – an image made by human design and skill. In the past God overlooked such ignorance, but now he commands all people everywhere to repent. For he has set a day when he will judge the world with justice by the man he has appointed. He has given proof of this to everyone by raising him from the dead.'

When they heard about the resurrection of the dead, some of them sneered, but others said, 'We want to hear you again on this subject.' At that, Paul left the Council. Some of the people became followers of Paul and believed. Among them was Dionysius, a member of the Areopagus, also a woman named Damaris, and a number of others.

Acts 17.19–33, NIV

Paul stands before a mixed hostile audience, with their own values and customs and little more than a faint interest in the gospel, and he wins some of them over. Note that some laughed at him, some rejected the gospel and yet some wanted to know more 'on this subject'. We should not worry that mission will at times bring us ridicule and criticism (even from within the ranks of the Church); we risk rejection for the sake of those who will want to hear more and believe. Follow the saints and preach the gospel!

Our tendency may be to speak of this work exclusively with young people, and yet once a month my parish hosts what it calls a 'Silver Service' – a fresh expression for the elderly and the isolated, many of whom have little other contact with the Church, either now or at any time in their lives. There wasn't any golden age when everyone went to church, and we are kidding ourselves if we believe that the gospel shouldn't reach out to everyone in our society. Interestingly, with a little modification, the same principle applies to this group as well, and a storytelling ministry works equally as effectively with older generations. It would, however, make the title of this book very unwieldy if we were to include that!

A significant influence has been the work of Rob Lacey whose *The Street Bible*, *The Liberator* and *Word on the Street*[5] have been hugely beneficial to me. Although we come from very different places under the umbrella of the Church, I hope the passion we both share for the living dynamism of God's holy Scriptures is visible.

All our Scriptures have come to us in translation, which affects both words and meaning. Scripture itself is a human effort inspired by God ('God-breathed') but ultimately the work of fallible humankind with different perspectives, experiences and preoccupations. To some it may be heretical to point this out, but to fail to remember the hermeneutic context of Scripture is to risk raising the Scriptures to a paper and ink idol which distracts from the God who is behind it all. God's word is most definitely present in the Scriptures, but we must be careful not to disregard the culture in which Christ stood, his heritage, lineage and cultures in which the accounts of God's work in the world took place. Two reports of a football match from two different commentators will always be different because of the difference in perspective on the match and team loyalty. In the same way, we should look beyond the words to see the Word (*logos*) behind it all.

For this reason, retelling sacred stories takes some liberties while drilling into (what this storyteller perceives to be) the truth behind them: to harness our heritage to be a platform for evangelism. Too often Scripture is seen as too precious an artefact to be a tool of evangelism when it really is our best

---

5 R. Lacey, *The Street Bible*, Zondervan, 2002; R. Lacey, *The Liberator*, Zondervan, 2006; R. Lacey, *Word on the Street*, Zondervan, 2002.

tool: the tool used by Peter and Paul and all the apostles and all the evangelists who have followed. It is the substance of our encounter with the living word of God made flesh. Treat your Scripture as dry and dusty, and your faith will appear the same.

Of course, this isn't an original take, and there is a movement of biblical storytelling which uses these classic dramatic and oral historical techniques to spread the gospel.[6] I would like to see this book as a small contribution to that movement. The stories themselves are designed for speaking aloud, and as such they are quite deficient in proper punctuation because people simply don't speak in perfectly formed sentences. Please forgive the inconsistencies of grammar and punctuation as I try to capture the breathless essence, the enthusiasm and the sense of awe and wonder which derives from a close encounter with the living God.

Naming Jesus

Even those who have no real encounter with the faith know of the word 'Jesus', even if only as a swear word. The only time Christianity appears to make the papers or the TV news is over controversy and falling out: the outspoken and adversarial positions of individuals on women bishops or sexuality or Sunday trading paints a Church and a faith which is more concerned with division than unity, with halting *anything* rather than pointing to a greater reality. 'Jesus' as a result still carries some cultural baggage, and not all of it is positive.

For this reason, when these stories began to be retold, I studiously avoided the name of the Lord and Saviour. I referred to 'the Man' (as in this programme) and only gradually introduced the revelation of his name, having introduced his Hebrew name. This has attracted some criticism: Was I ashamed of using his proper name? Did I have something to hide? Was I just trying to be cool?

My response would have to be that at the start, it just seemed right. Names in Scripture have meaning and they have power: names are changed to signify discipleship and transformation (Abram becomes Abraham, Jacob becomes Israel, Saul becomes Paul). The sacred name of God represented by the Tetragrammon (YHWH) is not spoken aloud, but substituted with names such as

---

6 www.wikipedia.org/wiki/Biblical_storytelling

LORD (signified by the capital letters). 'Jesus' is not the name that Our Lady Mary would have used to call him in for his tea, but rather his original and proper name 'Yahshua' – a name which has significance and meaning as 'Salvation' or 'God Saves'. Our Saviour's role was identified even in his naming! In the New Testament, he is rarely addressed as 'Jesus' but more commonly as 'Rabbi', 'Teacher', 'Master'. One notable exception to this is by the penitent thief[7] who asks, 'Jesus, remember me when you come into your kingdom.' I was leading a Bible study in a young offenders' institution and wondered aloud why this was an exceptional address. "S'easy – they spent the night in the same cell, didn't they?' they replied, and the experience of these young men and their Lord came into a profound new insight.

So, rather than begin my frontline evangelism by young people putting up barriers against the name of Jesus, I sought to create mystery and intrigue: Who is this man? From where does his power come? Turning back to Paul at the Areopagus, his missional speech doesn't mention Jesus either – just one whom God raised from the dead. It feels like a teaser, a desire for the people of Athens to ask for more, and it's always a good idea to model our mission on the saints. One of the problems we face is that people always expect the answer to be Jesus:

> One Sunday the priest was using squirrels to help him make some point on faith for the children. He started, 'I'm going to describe something, and I want you to raise your hand when you know what it is.' The children nodded eagerly.
>
> 'This thing lives in trees (pause) and eats nuts (pause) ...' No hands went up. 'And it is grey (pause) and has a long bushy tail (pause) ...' The children were looking at each other nervously, but still no hands were raised. 'It jumps from branch to branch (pause) and chatters and flips its tail when it's excited (pause) ...'
>
> Finally one little boy tentatively raised his hand. The priest quickly jumped for an answer. 'Well,' said the boy, 'I know the answer must be "Jesus" ... but it certainly sounds like a squirrel!'

Indeed, as comedian Stuart Lee pointed out, there are certainly some questions to which 'Jesus' *is* the answer:

---

7 Luke 23.42.

'Complete the name of this eighties band – The Blank and Mary Chain?'
'For what role did Robert Powell receive a BAFTA award?'

... and 'Who came into this world to save us?'[8]

The name of Jesus is powerful and certainly needs to be reclaimed from being simply a swear word, and with hope maybe we can turn 'OMG' into a real prayer.

The Programme

Describing this as a programme makes it appear meticulous and clearly thought out. In reality, the choice of story was largely drawn out of a desire to build an overarching narrative while responding to what was going on with the young people before us. In this way, you too should be prepared to move things around and, most importantly, inculturate your message for your young people: a rural community in New York State is different from one in Northumberland and different again from an urban one in south London: take these stories and make them your own, and having read this take on them, return to the original Scriptures from which they come – the fount of all.

There is an overarching narrative which stands out from the Gospels which cannot be achieved by digging deeply into individual lines, words or commas (the latter of which cannot be found in the original manuscripts) but must be experienced as a metanarrative. Ask yourself the question with every story: 'What is God trying to say *through* this story, not *in* this story?' When you consider these stories in this way, the outrageous message of love becomes clear, the minutiae of a story, so often overanalysed by erudition or biblical study, becomes less relevant to the word of God, hidden beneath all these words of God.

In telling stories of God, I find that they work best when they are told, rather than read. Some churches and communities which consider themselves to be 'biblical' throttle the life out of the narrative[9] in order to avoid any hint of drama or 'ritual' and yet these are dramatic stories, told by the most charismatic man to have walked the earth, retold in ways which were only

---

8 I set that question, not Stuart Lee.
9 L. Pierson, *Storytelling: A Practical Guide*, Scripture Union, 1997, pp. 91–125.

xii   FRONTLINE EVANGELISM WITH YOUNG PEOPLE

latterly put on paper and so existed primarily as an oral witness to the work of God. If you drain the Scriptures of their drama, you drain them of the vibrancy which has sustained them over two millennia. So, commit the story you are telling to memory, ideally from the original Scripture, and tell it like you were there. With this technique or approach you capture the immediacy of the Gospel of Mark, apply to it a modern edge or context: a location which might be known to your young people, and in situations which translate effectively from Judea to Jarrow, Galilee to Glasgow. The texts reproduced in this book are a suggested take on this contextual retelling, but you should inculturate it for your own target audience. No two groups of young people are exactly alike, and you should begin to get to know your young people as you begin this programme, modifying these words for your own context and, most significantly, your own charism, your style, your mojo.

What Equipment Do I Need?

The most important equipment you need is your interest in being committed to this mission, being up-to-speed on these stories and willing to put them out in front of young people who might not seem to have much enthusiasm for what you have to say. If you look at the text for the first time only a few minutes before you tell it and have to resort to reading it, then it will sound, frankly, dull.

You can show videos, play music to set the tone, and where these are mentioned, the book includes a QR barcode that you can scan to link you to the right YouTube or Vimeo video. Most smartphones can download a barcode reader app for this purpose.

QR codes are great fun, and can be very interactive and engaging, not in themselves but for where they lead: a treasure hunt around the church with QR codes which have to be scanned to find the next clue and location, or links to interesting videos or websites. This is a technology which is fairly new, but very common and easily recognized by young people (they are on many ads and billboards these days), and is one we can take advantage of creatively as well as being a foolproof way of publishing links. The codes can be generated very easily for free from sites such as www.qrstuff.com.

In an open setting, particularly one where only a few moments before the young people have been playing table tennis or messing around on a Play-

Station, it can be difficult to change the pace, to establish a sacred space. I sometimes try and achieve this with a video opener, or dimming the lights once they have gathered. It is much easier if you are able to take them into a new space: church is ideal, where the lights are low, the candles flickering and a sense of mystery and specialness can be sensed. Use your church if you can – it is a powerful space and you can set a wonderful sense of expectation. The simple act of movement into a different space, which has been previously set up and is ready to receive them, is a sort of mini-pilgrimage, a journey to do something different and special.

Some of the following sessions suggest other activities, for which occasionally other equipment might be necessary. Where it is, a list is given so you can get everything ready in advance. One thing to remember is that the young people will have been at school all week, and the last thing they want is another experience which feels like school.

Acknowledgements

Many of the activities and reflections have come about through discussions with my wonderful wife, Lorraine Rundell, and my good friends and colleagues, Vickie Williams, Elizabeth Burke, Dean Pusey, Fr Robb Sutherland, Mthr Ruth Innes and Fr Simon Cutmore. Each has given me good advice and insight, and many thanks are due.

Fr Wealands Bell is one of the funniest and most creative priests I have ever met. His writing is an inspiration to me, and some of his language and his humour have influenced many of these stories. I could not better his take on Peter, and so with his permission I have included it here.

Clare Williams is a Welsh artist with whom I have walked this spiritual journey for many years. Her Stations of the Cross were originally painted for the National Youth Pilgrimage to the Shrine of Our Lady of Walsingham in 2010. I love her art, and it is with much gratitude that she has given permission for them to be included. The originals are also available for use; please contact her on clarebear_e@hotmail.com

I have been involved in youth ministry for almost 20 years now. I have heard and shared so many stories and good ideas, created and adapted so many liturgies, forged my own work and appropriated so much from so many over the years that it all becomes a bit of a blur. Occasionally I have written something new and then later, checking it out, discovered that someone else had written something similar: this happens especially when we are drawing on the same scriptural materials. Where I have found these, I have noted them in the footnotes.

Lastly, I look towards the master storyteller of them all, without whom all is lost: all of this belongs to our Lord Jesus Christ, my master and redeemer from whom all these flow.

Prayers and Blessings

Fr. Simon

Simon Rundell

Plymouth, Devon
Candlemas, 2013

1

Who Is This Jesus?

Creation: Where it all comes from

John 1.1–18.

Introduction

It's impossible to gaze up at the sky and not wonder, 'Where did all this come from?' You can't observe a starlit sky or a sunset without some sense of awe and wonder. Even knowing that the sky at sunset is red because of pollutants in the atmosphere does not make it any less impressive. As science feels its way forward to the first moments of the big bang, it still hasn't captured the essence of it all, and there remains a sense that *something* is behind it all. However, we do know what that *something* is, not so much a thing as a beyond thing: God.

Preparation

Equipment: Either fridge-magnet words or an article or story from a magazine or newspaper cut into individual words.

Story

In the beginning there was nothing: nada, zip, zilch … not even chaos, which would at least have some form, even if it was … well … chaotic.

But beyond the nothingness, there was a something, even if we didn't have the words to call it anything. This something was a word – well, not just a word, but *the* word. The word of God spoken before all space and time, not shouted but whispered, a still, small voice amid … nothingness.

That word, that whisper spoken by God, was God: the same as God, which cannot be divided, or diluted, or mucked around with, it didn't matter how loud he had to speak it, because for God, just a whisper was enough, more than enough, and then springing out from the word, things happened and all creation was let loose.

That word had a name, the name we now know as Jesus – the Man, the Son of Man, the Christ, the Messiah, and when that word was said by God, things happened. That word, just a word, was life itself, more than just inert inorganic stuff, but life … life itself that lit up people's lives, a light that could shine into the darkest, scariest corners of existence and make it *good*.

There is no dark corner that this light cannot touch, nowhere that can't hear – somehow – the whisper of the word of God. It's in everything, through everything, with everything. It's the thing that glues the quarks together and makes the sun shine, the reason to get up in the morning and the reason to go to bed at night: the fingerprints of God are in all of creation, and the challenge is to spot it.

Activity: Cut up technique

Action: Mix up all the words you've cut out and lay them out at random. Note that although some sense might randomly come out, it doesn't make complete sense. We could continue to mess around with these words: swapping pairs of words or paragraphs of jumbled, meaningless babble, but it'll never be totally right. Try it and see.

Imagine this pile of words, and a mighty wind blowing through them like a tornado, whipping them up and, when they hit the ground, falling into the complete works of Shakespeare: imagine how difficult and unlikely this might be … and that's how likely that all of this world came together by accident, at random, that chemicals and amino acids collided together and made all this in its marvellous, wonderful diversity, and made all of you in your beautiful, random wonderfulness.

The truth is, I don't have enough faith to believe that all of this happened by accident: I don't have enough faith to believe that you are a random, freak accident, and so I have to conclude that something is behind it all, and that takes a lot less faith than believing in the random whirlwind.

Application: Faith isn't asking the impossible

We often think of faith and science as opposites, and certainly there are some who would like you to believe it's a black and white, one or the other kind of decision, and yet as with most things, faith and science overlap, merge, combine. Who do you think invented the lasers and the volcanos and the particle physics in the first place? The whole world contains the fingerprints of God, and the more science shows us, the more it shows us the handiwork of God. Hundreds of years ago a wise man by the name of Thomas Aquinas thought about God: how, if you thought of one thing happening, and then thought of the thing that caused it to happen, and then the thing that caused that to happen – like dominos toppling – if you go back and back and back until you run out of causes, *and then go back another one*, you are at the thing we call God: the 'first mover', the one who pushed the domino in the first place. Steven Hawking and many other scientists have touched on this issue, have explored the wonders of the first few nanoseconds of creation (or the big bang you might want to call it) and *still* haven't got close to the one who pushed the first domino. What was before? The Word. Let us try and hear that word and spot the subtle fingerprints of God on this marvellous universe.

Birth: Not a cute story at all

Matthew 2.1–12; Luke 2.1–20.

Introduction

St Francis of Assisi was the first Christian to provide us with the nativity scene: he did it so that the ordinary people of Italy where he lived could identify with the reality of that Christmassy image, to bring home to them the idea that the God who appeared to be so far removed from them might be one of them.

The problem is that it has all become so removed once again from our reality, and the image of squalor, of cold, of humiliation, has become a tranquil scene of calm. 'The cattle are lowing, the baby awakes, but little Lord Jesus, no crying he makes': heretical nonsense, for the baby was born, cried and messed his nappy. To think otherwise makes Jesus inhuman, and to make him inhuman makes a mockery of the incarnation. The challenge with this story is to unplug the incarnation – literally the *enfleshment* of God – from those cute images of Santa and Irving Berlin's *White Christmas*. This is an outrageous, radical and subversive idea, that God should step into his world, and it transforms us because God becomes one of us.

You can play the song 'What if God was one of us' by Joan Osborne. A good video perhaps can be found at:

or at http://bit.ly/YLZnqs

We sometimes overlook the scandal, the (for us) outrageously early age of 12 or 13 at which God asked this incredible thing of Mary, the dangers of child-birth, the long and risky journey and the refugee status that was to haunt the Holy Family for the first few years of the remarkable child's life.

Preparation

Equipment: Access to the internet. If you search Google for 'El Caganer' you will find lots of cheeky images. If you ever visit Catalonia, you might even be able to get a real one!

Story

It was a long, hard journey, not the kind of journey that should be undertaken by a man past his prime like me or the girl. From the moment I'd arranged this marriage with Joe, her father, I knew she was more than just a pretty little thing who'd look after me in my old age: she was gentle, faithful, caring … special.

Then, just before we'd finalized the wedding and everything, she tells me of this weird encounter with an angel, of all people, about a child that will be of God. A child? Of God? For me those days are over, and this is a quiet place, so imagine the scandal that would be caused around these parts: the gossip machine going into overdrive and all that talk behind my back. Still, I didn't want to cause any public disgrace, for me or her, I was just going to allow the engagement to slip away, quiet-like.

But then there was the dream. Not just like a night after too much cheese, more like a vision, a visitation. 'It was going to work out.' Trust in God. Trust in her. Trust. Unlike so many dreams that pass in the morning, this remained vivid: strong, powerful, reassuring.

So I decided to carry on, to make this work, to support her, and see how it would pan out. We coped during the pregnancy; in fact it was lovely, and although we were pretty poor, we scraped a living. It was going to be fine, and we just decided we could weather the sniggers and the gossip.

Then they threw it all up in the air by demanding this census: back home, days by foot to join all the rest originally from Bethlehem, the ancestral home of the Davidson family. It was all about the paperwork, and no doubt all about the tax they intended to bleed from us.

Travel with a girl who is about to drop a baby and you discover quite how tough this pregnancy thing is. It was a hard journey, but we had to go. Three whole days on the road, properly on the road, sleeping rough, risking bandits and cheaters. It seemed like the whole nation was on the move.

By the time we got to the village, it was dark, it was late, it was absolutely packed. No room. No chance. No time to lose, for this baby was on the way. Place after place was full, distant relatives unable to help, until finally, seeing the look of panic on my face and the imminent arrival of the baby, one of the keepers let us stay in the cave with the animals.

Even for people as poor as us, it was a bit of a comedown, but it was warm, dry and somewhere where the miracle could happen: the miracle of childbirth. I know it happens every day, every hour, but it still seems miraculous to me. So, surrounded by the animals, and all their poo, something special happened. It changed me, and it felt like it might change the world.

It wasn't anything like the images you see on the postcards: nice and fluffy and comfortable, a few animals and a nice clean stable – we don't even know what a stable looks like, we always keep our animals in the caves around these parts. Our lives were much messier: dirty, smellier and far less respectable.

The child was born into this dirty, smelly, unrespectable world; pretty soon these shepherds came knocking on the door. I know what you're thinking of, shepherds as honest, decent poor folk, but we never saw shepherds like that. Frankly, even poor people like us looked down on shepherds because they had to be outdoors in all seasons in all weathers, working on the Sabbath – the holy day of rest. They were a bit rough, a bit smelly, a bit outcast. But they came to the cave with tales of awe and wonder, a message from the heavens, a gift from God ... in the form of this small, vulnerable child.

If God chooses to work through the weak, the poor, the vulnerable ... look at him ... then what is respectable anyway? There's no shame any more. Not when there's a child in the world.

Activity: El Caganer

A New Zealand nativity from St Paul's, QR Code:

or at http://bit.ly/Wd2Lso

You can't resist this retelling because of the 'Ahhh' factor, and it's a good contrast to the dirty, smelly story you tell.

Catalonian cribs traditionally feature an additional character who sits (or rather squats) alongside the traditional characters of Mary, Joseph, shepherds and wise men. His name is El Caganer[10] and he is performing a normal, daily

---

10 http://en.wikipedia.org/wiki/Caganer

act: he has his trousers around his ankles and he is defecating. To spot this lovable little peasant among the calm and serene biblical characters is quite a shock, yet then we remember that the whole point of the nativity scene is to bring the incarnation back to our reality. Here is the truth: poo is incarnational, and – this shocking reality might upset the very pious – the baby Jesus soiled his nappy. Some expressions of faith pull so far back from the dirty, messy realities of life that they are in danger of removing the incarnated Christ from the world. Christ laughed, wept, joked, loved, drank and scandalized the religious around him because he was a part of this world: he knew hunger[11] and he experienced fear,[12] he was an asylum seeker and criticized as a drunkard and a glutton. Therefore we should always be looking for an El Caganer in our nativity scenes because that *everyman is us*.

Application

Incarnation means 'en-fleshment' – *carne* (as in chilli con carne) means meat. This is where God comes out to 'meat' … sorry, meet with us. Why? Because we matter, that's why. God's work in this world would have been done at a distance, but would have been done *to* us, rather than *with* us. The most outrageous part of this story is not the poverty or the poo, but that Almighty God should choose to step into our world and become enveloped in our reality: to come alongside us. On one level, it makes no sense, which is precisely why it is the wisdom of God.[13]

---

11 Matthew 4.1–11.
12 Luke 22.39–44.
13 1 Corinthians 1.25.

Discovered in the Temple: Light in the darkness

Luke 2.22–35.

Introduction

Candlemas marks the end of the Christmas season, and retells the story of the encounter in the great Temple in Jerusalem between the Holy Family (Joseph, Mary and the Christ-child) and an old man called Simeon. It is Simeon himself who retells this encounter and references his hymn of praise which is a mainstay of Evening or Night Prayer: the Song of Solomon (from the first two words in Latin of the Scripture *Nunc Dimittis*). The canticle speaks of promise and fulfilment.

The reason that the Holy Family had come to Jerusalem was to give thanks to God on the eighth day of Christ's birth, marking his circumcision and dedicating him to the Lord, as was the tradition of every firstborn son. The irony of dedicating God (in human form) to God (the Father) should not be lost on us. While the Temple stood (until AD 70), most Jewish worship was mediated through the sacrifice of animals, and the size and quality of the animal offered indicated your wealth. Pigeons were at the bottom of the social standing.

Preparation

Equipment: For the ritual you will need three large candles and a lighter. If you do not have a snuffer, then an effective way to blow out a candle with minimal wax spillage is to put your finger between the candle and your lips as though you were about to 'shhh' it. When you blow past your finger, the air goes round and puts the candle out on both sides without shedding wax everywhere.

Story

It's hard to describe just what the Temple was like: not like the churches of today with their hushed quiet, but more like a supermarket on Christmas Eve: chaos, people everywhere, the selling of the animals for the sacrifice, the money-changers, the people – the people.

I'd been a regular at the Temple for years … praying, praying, praying … faithful to God, witnessing to him, being part of the faithful old crew, alongside Anna and a few others. One evening I was praying and I sensed that God was very close. I just knew that his promise was true – the Messiah was coming and I would actually be a part of this … I would witness the one who would save Israel … all that praying paid off! What a privilege!

Of course when he tells you something like that, he never tells you *when*. I'm getting on a bit and this Messiah, the Saviour of the world, well, he'd better hurry up is all I can say.

So there we were in our favourite corner of the Temple, and as usual it was complete chaos, people everywhere, and I was looking across the courtyard and I spotted them: nothing special to look at really, just another poor couple … baby in their arms, coming in to thank God for their newborn. You see them all the time; they haven't got the money for anything more than a pigeon – richer people could afford better, like a dove or even a calf, but a pigeon was about the cheapest thing on the sacrifice menu. I could tell they were faithful people who wanted to thank God for the child, to dedicate him to the Lord as they say in our tradition.

I just knew. It was like a prompting in the pit of my stomach, a nudge in my back. This was it! Not what I was expecting. We'd always thought the Messiah would come down from heaven in a fiery cloud, chuck out the Romans, establish God's rule. This can't have been the plan, God's plan, it doesn't make sense. Then again, nothing God ever does makes sense in this world, at first … but it always seems to be right in the end. That's God's wisdom, I suppose.

So I hobble my way through the crowds (I told you I was an old man) until I get to them. You could see it in their eyes … what was this mad old man rushing towards us for? I just held out my hands and they put the child – only a few days old – into my hands. I suppose they just expected me to give the child a blessing, but oh no, it was the other way around … in my arms here *he* was blessing *me*. I was filled with a sense of fulfilment, of completion, that all my life I had been building up towards this moment.

So I looked up towards the heavens and praised God:

Lord, you've made it all come true as you promised, and my life is now complete: I am at peace because I have seen your chosen one, your messiah, your Christ. You have revealed your light in the world to all: Jews and non-Jews alike.

I was beaming as I handed the child back to the confused-looking parents. I knew that my days on this earth would not be long, but I wasn't worried about that: I'd seen the future, all wrapped up in this tiny child, and it was going to be bright …

Activity: The darkness always flees from the light

The world often seems like a dark, scary place: full of violence and fear, loss and loneliness. Yet Jesus said he was the light of the world: the light that shines in the darkness.

If you can, turn off the lights, or at least seek out a dark corner. Light a candle (a Paschal Candle is best, not only because it will be the largest candle in the parish, but because it is itself a symbol of Christ our Light).

Note how the darkness flees from the light. There is no darkness that can overcome the light. There is nothing too shameful, too painful that the light of Christ cannot overcome. It might feel very hard and difficult to notice the light, especially when your back is turned away from the light of Christ, or you are looking so inwardly that you don't notice it; but turn around occasionally and welcome the light into your life.

This Penitential Rite may be helpful.

Liturgy: Penitential Rite

Three large candles are lit.

Jesus is the light of the world. That light is in each of us, for Jesus is always with us.

When we do things that are wrong, when we hurt or damage our friends or families, our environment, or ourselves, the light of Jesus becomes dim in us. Let us remember those times, sort out our lives and know that God forgives us.

During each petition, at the words 'we bring darkness', one of the three candles is extinguished.

When we do wrong to our family and loved ones, we bring darkness into our lives.
Father, forgive.
Father, forgive.

When we do wrong to our world, we bring darkness into our lives.
Father, forgive.
Father, forgive.

When we do wrong to ourselves, we bring darkness into our lives.
Father, forgive.
Father, forgive.

May the risen Christ heal and restore us *(light candle)*
save us from all evil *(light candle)*
and give us his light always *(light candle)*
Amen.

Application

Light is a useful symbol for Christ, as it brings comfort and warmth, security and safety to an otherwise bleak existence. If we live dismal lives, in the darkness of a life without Christ, then it is easy to ignore our surroundings, our world and the needs of others. However, with even just a little bit of light in the darkened rooms of our lives we can see better the things which need our attention. The light of Christ enables us to see the needs of others as well as an examination of our own lives.

This is not something which should embarrass us or cause us anxiety or guilt, for the Christ who calls us to turn away from the dark and face the light does so with love, not condemnation. Seek his forgiveness, and it will be given to you; turn to the light, and feel the love.

When you find yourself alone and afraid (and even in faith there will be those times), light a candle and gaze into it in the quiet, and notice that it isn't quite so dark any more.

Lost in the Temple: Kids, eh?

Luke 2.41–52.

Introduction

Kids, eh? They always seem to be able to get themselves into trouble, run away, get themselves lost. Except, in this case it would appear to be not about getting lost, but being found: another glimpse of the nature of God-come-down-to-earth.

The story would appear to be missing huge chunks of childhood, teenage years and adulthood: from birth and refugee/asylum-seeker status to this story to, well ... nothing until his public ministry bursts onto the scene almost 20 years later. Isolated recollections, snapshots from what until then had been a largely ordinary life, apart from these glimpses of the amazing individual yet to be revealed. St John calls some of these glimpses 'signs' but doesn't speak at all about the child Jesus, and yet if signs are to point the way, here is a pointer to the greater things ...

Preparation

Equipment: For the game you will need to prepare a list of names of famous people: alive or dead, classical or current soap/pop stars, fictional, real, cartoons even!

Story

Annual trip to the big city for the national holiday. The usual round of visits to the Temple, seeing the distant cousins who'd come in from elsewhere. A bit of a catch-up, a bit of a party, a bit of the Passover ritual, a bit of political chat – these Romans, eh? And a gossip. Now it's time to head back to Nazareth and back to the workshop. Everything packed? Good. Off we go. Home's more than 70 miles away, so walking it will take us the best part of four days.

Where's the boy? Oh, he'll be with his mates, or his cousins, or someone else from my rabble of a family. I haven't seen him, but he'll be fine. You know what kids are like.

We sat down at the end of the first day's walk, and I tried to find him. Nowhere. 'Have you seen him?' 'No – I thought he was with you!' 'Where can he be?' It's 'Home alone' without the home – so I said to the missis, we're going to have to go back: against the tide of people swarming out of Jerusalem. 'You're going the wrong way!' they shouted. 'Have you forgotten something?' they joked. If only they knew, they'd understand the anxious faces we wore – he's only a child, not yet a man – at 12 he doesn't get that privilege until later in the year, and Jerusalem is a risky city, anything could happen to him … anything.

Three days he was missing. Three frantic, heart-aching days. I was at a total loss. We tried Straight Street, tried the square, the Roman Garrison in case he'd been arrested … nothing. There comes a time when there is nothing else for you to do but pray, so we went up the hill to the Temple.

There he was. Not lost. Not upset. Not hungry. In fact, he was in the middle of the teachers of the law, and even though he was just a lad, he was holding his own in the discussions with them: talking real theology, talking sense about the Scriptures … and I thought, 'Where *did* he get that from?'

Mary didn't pause to think about anything – she grabbed him and gave him the scolding of his life. 'What *were* you thinking? What are you doing here? Don't you know how worried we were?'

Calm as anything he just looked at us: no defiance, no shame: 'I was here. Doing the Father's business.'

I was about to open my mouth and protest: I'm a craftsman, not a priest, and then it struck me what he said – *the Father's* business, not mine. The Father of us all. He's going to do something important in the future. I don't know what it will be, but watch this space I suppose …

Activity: Belonging – the family game[14]

Jesus felt a deep and profound link to both his earthly and heavenly family. In the same way we belong to the family that raises and nurtures us as well as to the worldwide family of God nurtured by our loving creator. This game can

---

14 Fr Paul and Zena Matthews, two of my heroes in youth work, taught me this game and I am forever indebted to them for the game and, more importantly, for their inspirational ministry to young people in Sussex.

be played with as few as a dozen or as many as 50 young people. The brilliant thing is that in the end there are no losers!

You will hopefully have prepared your list of names for use in the game.

Go round to each person and secretly give them one of the names. They must not divulge it to anyone. I find that teenagers frequently forget who they have been given, so keep a record so you can remind them secretly. Depending on the group, either put the list up on a board or (harder) read out the list. Divide the players into at least four teams or families. Get them to stand in separate corners/areas.

The starting corner must select/remember a name and point to a family where they think s/he is residing, e.g. 'We think Bart Simpson is in that family.' If they are correct, that family member (Bart Simpson) must reveal themself and become adopted by moving to the family who guessed correctly. They have another go until they are unsuccessful in identifying a name in any of the other families. Play moves to the next family who, of course, will now know where Bart Simpson is, so they can start by asking him to come over to their corner. The more family members who are guessed, the greater the feat of memory for the guessing team. Eventually all the family members are revealed and everybody is called to the same family. This family is the winner – and everyone is in it!

Tip: the person leading the game should mark off their list as each family member is found. If there are a lot of players it is worth reminding them at regular intervals of who has not been found. It can take up to an hour, so have plenty of time!

Application

Relationships are key: the gospel you share will not wholly be won or lost on the power of your argument or the vigour with which you proclaim it, but on the relationships that you make and the disciples that you form. A church is not simply a body of worship or a confessional gathering, but a community in relationship with each other and with God.

What young people seek from you is support: acceptance, trust and love. They seek authentic community with people who they understand will be there for them, and not just when they give the 'right' answers.

Uncomfortable Realities:
The woman who bled

Matthew 9.18–22; Luke 8.43–48.

Introduction

The Old Testament is full of prohibitions, of 'thou shalt nots' and warnings of dire consequences for failure to keep within the boundaries. For the nomadic and then recently settled Jewish people, boundaries were essential: keeping those who weren't Jewish out. This is made even more clear by the 'Peace Wall' which surrounds the Palestinian territories today. These boundaries were not just physical, but cultural and spiritual as well. Rules of life and faith which could be attributed to the Canaanites or Philistines were prohibited (tattoos for example),[15] and things which smacked of ambiguity or mixing were an abomination, such as wearing clothes made of two fibres[16] or eating an animal which lived in the sea but could survive in the air.[17] Similarly, the cultish use of sacrifice made blood an especially powerful symbol of life and death. A bleeding woman, whether monthly or as a result of a gynaecological problem, as in the story below, was therefore something to be feared and shunned.

Even today, we shy away from talking about menstruation, even though plenty of studies show that not talking about this normal part of life for 50 per cent of the population causes anxiety, guilt and fear in young girls. The teaching of Leviticus 15.19–30 seems to run very deep in our society, even though it is normal. It is difficult to bring up these matters, particularly in a mixed group of young people, but if you treat it like a normal part of life, then perhaps they will too. Sensitivity and a straightforward approach will help you and them engage with this story without embarrassment.

---

15 Leviticus 19.28.
16 Leviticus 19.19.
17 Leviticus 11.10. It would appear that only some Levitical verses apply absolutely these days.

Preparation

Equipment: 5 feet/1.5m of string, a small crucifix, scissors and tape for each prayer rope. I advise practising the knotting in advance so you have one to show, and to help young people when they get stuck.

Story

Blood is feared: dangerous, dirty, the life force which is within each and every one of us. There are plenty of taboos in so many cultures about blood, and the Jewish faith is no different.

We'd come to the town of Caesarea Philippi, and the crowds were out in force. They'd heard so much about the Man that they just had to hear for themselves: that teaching, that healing, the difference that just a word or a smile in your direction would make to your inner feeling.

We were basking in the reflected glory of being with him. The times when we were laughed at, threatened, had the dogs set on us or had to sleep rough seemed to be a thing of the past as the people started to notice the difference he made to their lives.

The crowds were now immense, pushing in from every side, trying to get a glimpse, get a blessing, get a piece of the action. We did our best to stop him and us from being crushed, but it was a tough task. They don't give you a high visibility jacket and an earpiece to be one of his bouncers; you just have to try and control the crowds as best as you can.

In the midst of all this pushing and shoving, shouting and calling, he just stops. He turns.

'Who touched me?'

Well, the crowd was everywhere, a bit of human contact was unavoidable, inevitable really.

'No, who touched me? I felt that particular touch,' he said.

The crowd became really uneasy, ashamed even. Then a little old woman shyly raised her hand …

'It was me, master, I'm really sorry. I've been ill for so long, so tired, so unwell. The bleeding has been going on without stopping for the past dozen years. I knew that if I could just touch the hem of your prayer shawl, there would be healing, there would be my salvation in it, just like the prophet Malachi said.'[18]

---

18 Malachi 4.2 – the same Hebrew word for 'wings' is 'corner' or 'fringe' – some suggest

Bleeding? Ugh! That made it really dirty, nasty, horrible. That woman shouldn't be out in public. Sharing the same market square as her made me feel dirty. There's something about blood which makes me feel a bit sick. The thought of her touching him made me feel unwell, and as far as the religious authorities were concerned she would taint you with her dirtiness. Ugh!

But that didn't seem to bother the Boss. As she shyly admitted her outrageous act, his face changed. It was full of care, concern: the blood and the dirtiness didn't worry him.

'As soon as I touched you, I felt it was different. I feel different.'

'You are,' he said, matter-of-factly, 'your faith has healed you.'

Her rude act, to touch where she had no right to touch, was an act of faith: by reaching out to him she saw as the prophet Micah saw, that the Messiah was here. He had come from the fringes of Israel, the backwater of Nazareth, the poor carpenter's son, and in the fringes of his prayer shawl the Messiah's healing was made clear.

Reach out for the Messiah. You might not physically make contact with his fringes, but you will encounter the same love, the same healing. Reach out, and do not be afraid how dirty you feel, how unworthy. Reach out and encounter Christ's healing.

Activity: Prayer ropes

The fringes which the woman touches are traditional tassels (or *tzitzit*) on the Jewish prayer shawl (*tallit*). They are often knotted and so remind me of Orthodox prayer ropes. Making traditional prayer ropes is very complex and quite difficult, so here are some instructions for making Western rosaries using knots.

---

that this refers both to the salvation or healing which comes from the hem of the tallit and the fringe of Israel which is Nazareth.

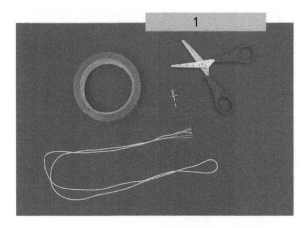

You will need approximately 5 feet or 1.5 metres of twine to make a single decade rosary, a couple of small pieces of tape, and a crucifix.

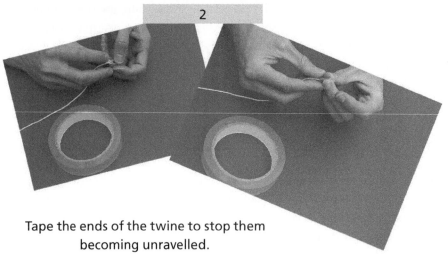

Tape the ends of the twine to stop them becoming unravelled.

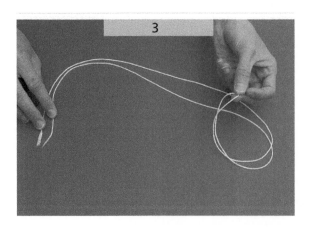

Divide the twine into two. This middle point will be the middle knot of your single decade rosary.

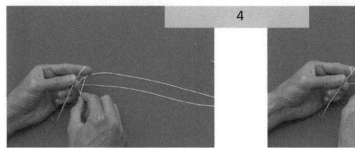

Loop the twine around your finger and cross it over.

Continue this loop and go round three times, looping towards your left hand.

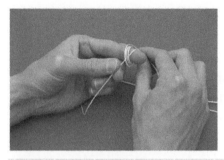

Try not to tangle the loops as it will make the knot neater.

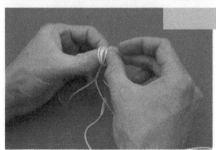

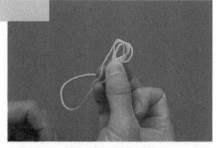

Carefully pull the loop towards the end of your finger.

Hold this loop in your right hand.

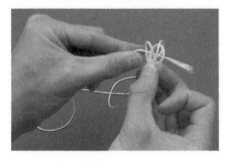

Thread the side you have just wound around from the left through the loops.

6

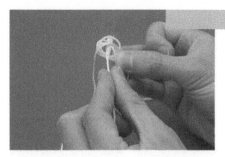

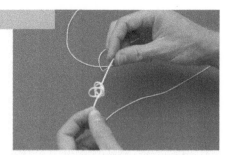

Carefully pull them together …

… so it forms a neat knot.

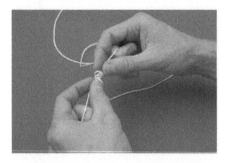

You might need to fiddle with it to
ensure it knots nicely and later on
move the position of the knot so
they are evenly spaced.

7

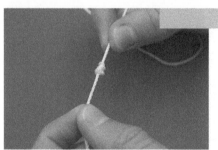

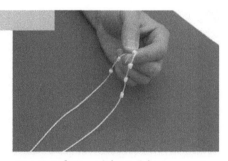

Your first knot!

Repeat from either side to create
evenly spaced knots.

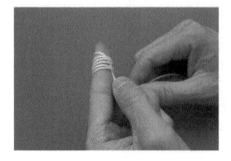

Make ten of these three loop
knots radiating out from either
side of the middle for each *Hail
Mary*. At each end, make a knot
with five loops for the *Our Father*
and the *Glory Be*.

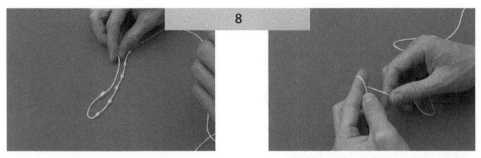

8

Take both ends and make a five-loop knot with both ends. This is the knot which joins the circlet together.

Continue to make knots down the two strands for the *Glory Be*, *3 Hail Marys* and the *Our Father*.

At the end use the ends to tie the crucifix to the rosary, and now you will have made your own rosary!

Application

Prayers useful for use with the rosary:

Apostles' Creed

I believe in God the Father Almighty, Maker of heaven and earth: And in Jesus Christ, his only begotten Son, our Lord:
Who was conceived by the Holy Ghost, born of the Virgin Mary: Suffered under Pontius Pilate; was crucified, dead and buried: He descended into hell: The third day he rose again from the dead:
He ascended into heaven, and sits at the right hand of God the Father Almighty:
From thence he shall come to judge the living and the dead:
I believe in the Holy Spirit, the holy catholic church: the communion of saints: The forgiveness of sins: The resurrection of the body and the life everlasting. Amen.

Lord's Prayer

Our Father,
Who art in heaven,
Hallowed be Thy Name;
Thy kingdom come,
Thy will be done,
on earth as it is in heaven.
Give us this day our daily bread,
and forgive us our trespasses,
as we forgive those who trespass against us;
and lead us not into temptation,
but deliver us from evil. Amen.

Glory Be

Glory be to the Father, and to the Son and to the Holy Spirit:
as it was in the beginning, is now, and shall be for ever, World without end.
Amen

Hail Mary

Hail Mary full of grace, the Lord is with thee.
Blessed art thou and blessed is the fruit of thy womb, Jesus.
Holy Mary, Mother of God, pray for us sinners now and at the hour of our
death. Amen.

Start at the cross: it all begins and ends with the cross. Make the sign of the
cross and say the **Apostle's Creed**.

At the first knot, say the **Lord's Prayer**, moving on to the next knot when
you have finished. At the next three knots, say three **Hail Marys** and at the
last knot on this straight piece of rope say the **Glory Be**. You should now be
at the circlet of ten knots.

As you think of the mystery you have chosen to pray, say the **Lord's Prayer**,
then ten **Hail Marys** followed by a **Glory Be**. You can repeat this five times,
reflecting on each mystery.

Although it feels difficult to begin with, you find that by getting your conscious mind to repeat these familiar prayers, your subconscious mind is able to pray freely, reflecting on those holy mysteries and truly engaging with God. It isn't a 'party' tool, belonging to a particular Church or tradition, just a good way of praying *alongside* the company of heaven.[19]

This is a link to a useful explanatory video (which explains the Mysteries of the Rosary):

or this link http://bit.ly/ZE3ObP

Wind and Waves: Ask

Mark 4.35–41.

Introduction

'Place your faith in Jesus', those cute little graphics posted on Facebook proclaim. Nothing wrong with that, but Jesus isn't going to remind you to brush your teeth in the morning or pick the winning lottery ticket for you. If you abrogate all responsibility for your actions then what will follow will be frustration and disappointment. Blame all your failings on the work of the enemy and you are diminishing your humanity, your created loveliness. Trust in Christ for the bigger picture, be sure of your heaven-bound destination, the

---

19 An unfounded criticism of the rosary is that it is prayer *to* Mary. This could not be further from the truth: all prayer is directed towards God, but we recognize that we pray alongside the angels, saints, prophets, patriarchs and, yes, our Blessed Lady. Never *to*, unceasingly, *with*.

assurance of sins forgiven; but like the disciples, understand that it's you who has to work out the next step. There are clues: the words of Scripture, the lives of the saints, the guidance of other Christians; but none of that tells you which shirt to wear tomorrow.

Preparation

Equipment: Dissolving paper (also known as 'spy paper') can be purchased on the internet or from any magic shop. They usually come in approximately A6 size and I always halve that to make it go further. If you don't have access to the church's font, then a large tub from a garden supplier is a good substitute and can be used for many water-based rituals – just make sure it doesn't have a hole at the bottom!

Story

'Come down to the lake,' he said. He was the only one among us who seemed to have a clue about why we were there or where we were going, but if there was one thing this 'following' had taught, it was that sometimes you had to trust that it would work out.

It appeared we had a destination, a direction, a course. There always had been one; even if most of us in our group hadn't really worked it out, content to just follow. The next step was clear: to the other side. There was a cabin at the back, and he, who had been teaching and healing non-stop for weeks, went straight to the cabin and went off to sleep, exhausted. The rest of us, pleased for this short break, just sat around on deck, chilling out. The sun was shining,[20] not a cloud in the sky. God was in his heaven and we were simply happy to be alive, in this place. We travelled serenely on our set course, towards our destination. The lake was as smooth as glass, the wind was gentle, and we felt marvellous; and I thought to myself as we skimmed lazily over the water how I never wanted this to end: sheer bliss.

---

20 In Mark 6.39, the evangelist notes that they sat down on the 'green grass'. On one level it is an inconsequential detail, but in others it is remarkable: this is an account from one who clearly was there and remembered it: a detail which stuck in the mind and has been transmitted to us over millennia. It adds authenticity to the account.

Almost as soon as I thought that, it all started to change: those wispy clouds started to thicken and that gentle breeze started to rise and the sky started to darken – the weather can close in around the lake really quickly, whipping over those Golan Heights, and before we knew where we were, we found ourselves in the middle of a storm – too far to go back and find shelter, we were committed to going forward, committed to the oncoming storm.

Well, the rain fell, the wind blew and the waves rose and we started to look a bit worried at the waves coming in over the side, and even, dare I say it, swamping us. This was no joyride now – it was getting serious. We were getting blown off course – now I feared we'd never make our destination.

The storm blew more and we started to fear for our lives – and where was he? Why wasn't he on deck with us? Why wasn't he telling us exactly what to do, why wasn't he keeping us right on to our hoped-for destination, why wasn't he telling us how to cope … but there he was, still asleep, apparently not caring or not aware of our impending doom.

I shook him awake. 'C'mon, we're drowning! Set us a course, tell us how to get to port. Shall we abandon ship, leap overboard and take our chances, find a different course … WHAT SHOULD WE DO?'

I was in a complete panic, and as I shook him, he opened just one eye to see me, soaked to the skin, seeing the sheer terror in my eyes. He, however, remained calm, very calm, disturbingly calm.

'Be calm,' he said to me and, raising his head a little, he glanced up at the sky and said …

'Shhh.'

Very quietly. He didn't raise his voice, he didn't need to, for there was a calm authority in his voice which didn't need volume.

'Shhh.'

And it went quiet. It went calm. And all that rage and fuss, and all that fear which went with it, went away.

'You can carry on now,' he said as he rolled over and went back to sleep, and we could stop, take stock and continue on to our final destination.

In my fear I called out to him, in my lost-ness I sought him out and he calmed things for me and in me before letting me get to my destination and complete my journey.

How can he have such authority? How can he have such power that even the storms of life become calm before him? How can he have such power that he wields it gently and without fuss to take away my fear? … because I asked him.

Liturgy: Dissolving paper

In order to give over to God things which batter us in the storms of life, the following liturgy uses dissolving paper. People are encouraged to write their confession or prayer on a small piece of this special paper and then place it in a body of water: it might be a river outside, or a large tub of water or (even better) the church's font. On contact with the water the paper dissolves and we can be assured that God washes away that which we want to confess, just like baptism.

There are many things that we would like to discard,
To throw away and have nothing more to do with.

There are many things which we feel are not worthy of us
And need to be put aside.

Write down something you want deeply to throw away:
A behaviour.
An action.
A word said in haste.
A relationship gone bad.
A deed undone.
An obligation unfulfilled.

And give it over to God.

You can pour out your heart to God on the mountaintop.
You can painfully trace each step in the darkness of the confessional.
You can say the words we know so well without thinking.
But have you written him a love letter?
Have you given what you want to throw away to God?
Let God deal with your deepest fears and shame.

Write down something you want deeply to throw away:
A behaviour.
An action.
A word said in haste.
A relationship gone bad.

A deed undone.
An obligation unfulfilled.

And give it over to God.

There are many things that we would like to discard,
To throw away and have nothing more to do with.

There are many things which we feel are not worthy of us
And need to be put aside.

Put them aside, and give them to God.

For God will transform,
and the shameful past becomes the bright future.

The text can be spoken as the activity takes place, or perhaps consider this video:

or click this link: http://bit.ly/UYia2Q

Application

Our approach to prayer is many and varied, and there is no 'right' way to pray. The legacy of prayer at school – hands together, eyes closed – often results in a narrow and outcome-orientated approach to prayer, like making a shopping list. It relies on us asking God for stuff, but not listening for the reply.

God listens to us all the time, not just when we have to attract his attention. To *pray without ceasing*[21] as Paul encouraged us to do involves recognizing that God is in all. If we are attentive enough we might be quite surprised by what he is saying to us. Prayer doesn't just happen when we are in a tight spot, like a shipwreck, but throughout our lives and even more before we even set sail on life's journey.

John Newton, the author of 'Amazing Grace', that well-known eighteenth-century song of redemption, was rescued from the shipwreck of the slave ship he was on. It was a transformation for him. You don't need something quite so blindingly obvious do you ...?

Peter's Faith: Follow me

Introduction

I love St Peter; he represents me in all the Bible stories: enthusiastic, not terribly clever, prone to opening his mouth and putting both feet in it. I have hope because of St Peter, and if Christ forgives him on the beach after the resurrection, then there is hope for me yet.

Preparation

Equipment: Gather pictures of famous people: from Mahatma Gandhi to Dr Martin Luther King, Nelson Mandela to David Beckham, a favourite local schoolteacher and one of your youth leaders. You can print them out or put them into a slideshow to project them on a wall or display them on a TV.

---

21 1 Thessalonians 5.17.

Death of a Rock: the Martyrdom of St Peter

by Fr Wealands Bell[22]

St Peter is in his cell, awaiting the guards who are to lead him to his execution and martyrdom. This monologue was written with the accents and dialect of the North East of England in mind. People from other parts of the country will need to amend the script in order for their own voices to be heard coherently. This was first performed by the author at the Youth Pilgrimage to the Shrine of our Lady of Walsingham on 10 August 2004. The words attributed to our Lord in the garden are Othello's rather than St John's. I've always thought that Shakespeare must have had the Lord's arrest in mind when he wrote *Othello* Act 1 Scene 2, and, as usual, his words are better than most others'. The reference to IKEA and cars with vavavoom should be changed when those phrases are no longer indicative of the extent of people's desires and their enslavement to advertisers.

They shouldn't be long now, like.

I'm excited. I really am. I know it's not everybody's cup of tea. But, like I said, I'm really looking forward to it, actually.

He said it would happen. Or at least, he hinted at it. Oh aye, he was a great one for the hint, for the peculiar promise. I'll be with you till the end of time, he said. Whoever eats me will live for ever.

I'm Peter, by the way. Truth is, I didn't know what he was on about half the time. I wasn't a bit like Martha and Mary and Lazarus and them. To be honest, I wasn't a great one for religion. But I certainly knew what he meant when he said there'd be no more late-night fishing, no more expeditions to fill the nets with flatfish, with juicy trout or a good leggy octopus. 'Follow me,' he said, and you will catch a shoal of souls. So I followed him. I thought he probably wanted a job doing, a bit of a hand to shift something to the other side of the water, or to help him with a bit of heavy lifting. At the finish, I asked him. We were getting nowhere quickly, and we kept on meeting more and more people who he'd tell to, you know, follow me.

'Where are we going?' I asked him. 'We're goin' nowhere fast.' 'Where on earth are you taking us?' I said. 'To my father's house,' he said. And smiled one of his smiles. I wish I could see one of them now. But it'll not be long.

The fact that he could cure people, heal them of diseases and that … That was the real giveaway. I mean, you'd expect the clergy and people like that to talk about heal-

---

22 Reproduced with permission.

ing ('I'm a priest! Let me through! I can help you …') but there's practically none of them that can actually do it. But by God, he could. By God he could.

We did all sorts in the end. Cripples, demoniacs, deaf, dumb, blind. Hunchbacks, lunatics, all of humankind! He even cured my mother-in-law once. I think I must have been in the other room, like, 'cause he'd done it before I could stop him.

And you know, he was always getting up the noses of the high priests, and that snotty lot who think they're better than the rest of us. He was always going for his dinner with somebody or other they looked down on: the immoral, the indecent, the unwashed, the unsound. They couldn't wait for him to take a tumble.

We ate with all sorts of people, conmen and frauds, the mad and the bad, taxmen, traitors, tarts. And wherever he went, there was a change: even simple water began to taste of wine, and a little lad's picnic was a feast of fine food for anyone who wanted it. He filled our veins not just with new wine, new blood: he gave us new life. And I could heal because he did. He let me heal others. (Aeneas. He was one. Funny fellow, but I healed him.)

Now, you know, I'll tell you something. I'm not a clever man; never was. I was once arrested for preaching because I was 'an ordinary and uneducated man'. Good job they've dropped that law! I never went to school, and I can neither read nor write, but little by little I began to understand something. And even when I understood nothing, I kept following, always following, because there was never a dull moment. And anyway, I knew that I'd never felt like that before. I mean, don't get me wrong, I'd had a good life till I met him. I was a big lad, popular, hard worker, always had a bit of cash for a bottle of wine or a game of dice. I had my fair share of lasses as well, till the wife finally put a stop to it. It was a good life, with plenty of storms and scraps and arguments to stop you getting bored. But all that was just me. My life was just filled with me. My story. My life. My concerns. I realize now that I had nothing till he came along. I needed a lend of his eyes, so that I could begin to see just how staggering, stunning, amazing, unbelievable is the God I'd been brought up to believe in.

Sometimes, of course, you'd get the answer to a question right, and then you felt like a million dollars! Like that day when he asked us who we all thought he was, and I got the right answer. You are the Christ, I said, the Messiah. And he told me I was blessed. Blessed are you, Simon bar Jonah, he said (Jonah, that was my father) … Mind you, he also said I couldn't possibly have worked out the answer for myself, and I think he was probably right.

But there was terrible times, as well, and I mustn't try to diminish them. Yes, I kept on following him, but the journey has never been without the odd diversion. It was as if the minute I got something right, I immediately got something horribly wrong. Like that time he called me blessed. It was only a few seconds later he was telling me I was worse than the devil. I can't remember what I'd said, now, but his words didn't half hurt, like a knife. I suppose I thought I could do things by myself, do them without him. I've always been independent. But it never pays off. He had this thing he could do, this walking on water. I tried it myself once. I knew he was carrying me along, so I tried to do it by myself, without him. I started to sink faster than you could say water wings, crushed under my own weight!

Young John likes the story of the garden. It was the night he was arrested, when that [here Peter struggles not to call Judas by a rude name] … when Judas fetched the priests to arrest him. I wasn't having that. I wasn't going to be called Satan again … I had my knife out of my belt and started to hack away at one of them. Chopped his ear clean off. Again, bad move, apparently. I thought I was doing the right thing, but he wasn't very happy with me. Keep up your bright swords, he said, for the dew will rust them. His mother landed me a clout to the back of me head I'll never forget. You're nothing but a great big eejit who spends too much time talking when he should be listening. That's what she said. Them Nazareth lasses can be fiery.

You'll be wanting to know about the crowing of the cockerel, the most famous alarm clock in the history of the world. Cock a doodle do! Cock a doodle do! … I hadn't meant to deny that I knew him. It was just that the barmaid had a gob on her like Solomon's portico, and the place was crawling with priests and coppers. There was no point in getting myself into trouble for it. I mean, there was nothing I could do to help him at that stage. So I said the words I've regretted ever since. 'Jesus? No, pet. Never heard of him. Not me. You've got the wrong man. I don't know any Jesuses.' If it's any consolation, I've regretted it ever since. But you see, it's like I said, I'm not really sainthood material: I get easily distracted, easily put off. [sings] *Mine eyes have seen the glory of the coming of the Lord*, but I sometimes like to forget that I've seen what I've seen, that I know what I know. D'you know what I mean?

One more minute, and then they'll be here. I won't get a chance to say much more. I'll be freed from all that, from the need to be like the Pope and have an opinion on everything.

And what would I say to you, dear friends, as you begin your life and I end mine? Just this: trust in God, and dare to imagine that there's more to life than trips to IKEA and cars with vavavoom … There is joy to be had from stuff which doesn't plug into the mains. The secret is to try to see everything through his eyes, and then it all looks very different.

You know, I never told Mark this when he wrote the story down, but I really didn't know what Jesus meant by 'Follow me'. I suppose I just knew that somehow, some distant day, I would discover what life had been leading up to. I think I'm about to find out.

Itchy palms. Itchy feet. Follow me.

Activity: The gift of ourselves

We all have gifts we can bring to God, although like Peter we might have no idea what those gifts might be. Those gifts might not feel to us very saintly at all, but God will use them all.

Put your images on the wall or up on a screen. Identify some of their attributes[23] and see how these attitudes, skills and achievements have made a difference to others.

Place a box with a slot in the middle of the top and invite everyone to note on a piece of paper what gifts, skills and attributes they have and contributions they make to the lives of others. Self-conscious teenagers can be particularly negative about themselves and can therefore need much encouragement. Invite them to think about the others in their group, and pick an attribute about someone else – often something that the individual might not readily choose themself or even be aware of.

You can fold the papers and place them in the box, offering them in prayer

Heavenly Father,
You have created us and wonderfully made us
A reflection of you.
For all that we are,
For all that we might become,
May we see others as you intend them
And see ourselves as you would have us be.
Inspire in us gifts that we are not even aware of yet.
You alone know the plans you have for us in this life,
Guide us in our paths
and bring us to that place where we will see each other
face to face, in your power and glory.
Amen.

---

23 One of the most touching things I have ever seen was to build up the confidence and self-esteem of a class which was always belittled as never likely to amount to much. Each day a different person was sent out of the class to return the register to the office, and while they were out of the room, the remainder of the class chose attributes of that person that they wished to celebrate and be thankful for. On their return, they were told all the wonderful things their classmates thought of them. Even the quiet and under-confident ones, I could see, shone through this appreciation. Mr Kupersamy – you work wonders with children.

You don't have to open the box then and there. How interesting might it be to open it at the end of the year, or even a few years down the road!

Application

Thanks to a number of largely fanciful biographies, the lives of the saints can often seem a little unreal: men and women with their heads in the clouds, divorced from reality and granted almost superhuman qualities. Scripture pulls no such punches: the disciples squabble among themselves, they say stupid things, and when the going gets really tough, they lie to save their own skin. They change their minds in the light of new thinking and new experiences of God – a most saintly quality which appears to be missing from modern political and church leadership – and they are open to the outrageous possibilities of God. In real life, saints must have been difficult people to live with. I am sure that St Francis or St Teresa of Avila were really infuriating, passionate, driven people filled with a down-to-earth love which comes straight from God to the people they encountered on their life's journey.

Young people, indeed all of us, should be encouraged to lead saintly lives – not to be removed from society and culture, but to engage in it and to transform it. With love.

The Incredulity of Thomas:
Faith seeking understanding

John 20.19–31.

Introduction

Faith is not like Jenga, the game where blocks of wood are removed from the base and placed on the top until it becomes a tottering tower ready to fall. If one of the blocks of faith is removed, it does not necessarily mean that the whole thing has to fall. If you have problems with some aspect of the Church's teaching or a difficult bit of Scripture, then it doesn't mean that God is going to cast you outside the Church for evermore.[24] Life is shades of grey and glorious colours, and a Church which tries to polarize it into black and white is missing out on the beauty of creation, the variety of life and the complexity of God's real world, filled with real human beings.

Preparation

Equipment: If you search the internet for images of 'Photoshop celebrity before and after' you will find a host of famous people who have been altered to satisfy the media's desire for stick-thin models and actresses without wrinkles. Take some of these images and stick them on each side of a bit of card. Add in some unretouched photos.

Story

Of all of his followers, I suppose I was the most literal-minded, which was a bit of an issue between me and him, I suppose. He always spoke in metaphors and images and loved to compare the things of God to things we could get a grasp on. I suppose it was my architect's mind at work here – you can't build buildings on metaphors, they quickly crumble and fall.

Well, my commitments had taken me away from the rest of the group that day, I needed to get over the blow of his terrible loss to us, and as we all deal with grief in different ways, I threw myself into work, as many do. So when I returned to the community that night they were buzzing with excitement: the stories were true, and he was alive! They had seen him in this very room, and he had appeared to them.

Yeah, right, was my response. Delusion, that is what I thought. Yes, Jesus was amazing, yes I saw some amazing things, miracles possibly, but back from the dead? No, surely not. My brothers and sisters were most adamant that they had actually seen him.

Listen, I'm not going to believe it unless I see it for myself. Unless I can place my fingers into the holes in his hands, put my hand into that wound in his side, I'm not going to believe. Like many, I need proof!

So, it was about a week later when we were all together, redoing what he told us to, sharing bread and wine to bring him into our presence, and then he was … really was!

---

24 Some in the Church might want to do that, but that is the Church, not God. The Church is the people of God, not a single institution, and is much bigger than the building or the hierarchy you meet in.

The doors were locked, and he didn't sneak in, but this was no ghost. I don't know how he got in, because we'd made sure it was secure. Standing in front of me was the very man I'd denied earlier in the week. 'Come,' he gently said to me, and he grasped my hand, leading it to his side. And I did. I put my hand into that sacred wound: I did something that if I pause to think about it was quite disgusting, but at the time seemed so special, so significant, so intimate; as though he wanted me to become linked with him. I examined the holes those nails made in his hands, saw the damage on his brow made by that cruel crown of thorns. It was real.

All I could do was fall to my feet before him, in awe, in adoration, in worship, because for the first time, after these three years of following him, after all the things I'd witnessed, only now did the reality finally dawn on me …

'My Lord, and my God,' I exclaimed. It was all I could say. It was the truth.

'Tom, you are blessed because you have finally seen what was in front of you, but there will be even greater blessings for those who believe without seeing.'

It's true, not everyone will get to see what I have seen, not everyone will get to experience Jesus in such an up-close and personal way, and yet this story is far too important for us to keep to ourselves. I need to tell others, to get John to write it down for me, and to ensure others don't fall into the same cynical trap I fell into: first-hand experience is good, but it doesn't mean that the truth, the real truth, isn't also out there, just beyond our senses; and God's truth often goes beyond those senses.

Blessed are those who believe without seeing … do you believe?

Activity: Real or Photoshop?

You can't always believe what you see. In the olden days, they used to manipulate photographs and remove people who had fallen out of favour with the authorities. Today we have Photoshop and other image manipulation software which can manipulate any image with digital precision.

Display or hand round some of your 'before and after' manipulated images. Ask your young people whether they think these images are real or manipulated. This can lead to a discussion about whether it is right to do this, and further, whether the young people feel pressure to be 'size zero' thin or have 'sixpack' muscles.[25]

---

25 Certainly the main pressure is on girls and their body image, but I have also found young men feeling inadequate because of the images of 'perfect' abs. None of this is right. If the temple has a little moss, that's not a problem in God's eyes.

This video *Beautiful* sets Christina Aguilera's haunting tune to some impossibly beautiful images of models and paragons of beauty. Amid all that eye candy, one cannot help but think, is this right?

Or this link: http://bit.ly/W0vodh

In 1 Samuel 16.7 the Lord says to his prophet, 'Man looks on the outside, but God looks on the inside.' What is within you is more important than your haircut or your trainers or your (absence of) spots. Young people may recall editions of *Britain's Got Talent* or the *X Factor* when the most unlikely people take the stage and prove themselves to be a thing of beauty.[26] God knows the beauty even inside someone who doesn't sing; he knows of what you are made and he loves you for it. 'By your fruits you will be known' says Jesus in Matthew 7.16. The way we treat others matters more than our outward appearance or our voice.

Application

Some doubt is okay. It is good to explore matters of faith and the theology that tries to work it through. All Scripture is trying to work out what God means, rather than, as some will dogmatically tell you, what God is. Do you think the awesome majesty of God can be trapped between the pages of a little book? Scripture is revelation, and is good, but is only part of the story. Some people can believe directly (and Jesus himself praises them) and others need to explore it a bit more. It doesn't make you any less of a Christian. Asking questions of faith is similarly not unbelief (for Thomas and Our Lady and Jacob and Moses asked questions of God) but the application of our God-

---

26 2009's Susan Boyle or 2012's Jonathan Antoine spring to mind.

given intellect to speaking of God.[27] You are not required to leave your brain at the door to church.

St George: A saint without need of a dragon

Introduction

St George is a popular saint across Europe: the patron of Georgia and Iraq, Egypt and Catalonia as well as England. He wasn't English and he clearly had never even been near England. This is worth remembering when some try to use his flag (the red cross on a white background) for their own political purposes. However, what he really stands for is worth celebrating.

Preparation

The only equipment needed for this story are Bibles, pens and sheets of paper.

Story

My name is Marcellus – if you want to know the whole name, rank and number thing, it's Marcellus Flavius, Forward Principal Legionnaire of the 31st Legion. I'm a soldier of more than 15 years standing and I've served throughout the empire, from the cold and barbaric moors of Britain down to Egypt. I've got one of those massive spears or pilum and when we work as a team, well there is nothing – nothing I tell you – that can break such a disciplined unit as ours.

We're commanded by a Tribune: an officer who's seen some action in the past and knows how to handle both us and anything we run into. His name is George from

27 Literally *theology* means 'speaking of God'. Theology is not therefore cut off from faith, but is an essential part of human discourse, and everyone – absolutely everyone – is invited to the conversation!

Lydda in Palestine. Despite what some people say, he wasn't ever with us in Angle-Land, never visited the place, but I like him: he's a good soldier and a strong leader of men.

They say that in the heat of a battle, when the arrows are flying overhead, you'd be hard pressed to find a man who doesn't believe in God: looking out for your survival certainly brings home the need for a higher power. Most of the time, the powers that be don't care what we worship, as long as it doesn't interfere with good discipline.

In recent years, some of the boys have been talking about that Jewish group which has opened up for everyone. It sounds a bit bloodthirsty to me, as they talk about peace and love and forgiveness and then they eat the flesh and blood of their leader. Ugh.

Still, the lads who've picked up that religion seem to like it; it makes them a bit … calmer, I suppose. I even heard that our own boss, George, had taken it up. It's a nice little religion, I understand, doesn't do any harm to anyone and wants people to be nice to one another. Nice.

Some of our emperors have, recently I have to admit, taken to getting ideas above their station: imagining themselves as gods, demanding to be prayed to, to have statues and temples and to receive sacrifices. They seem to have forgotten that they are mortal. Diocletian the current emperor seems to have it worst: he *hates* them Christians as they call them. I hear that in some areas he has tried to have any Christian soldiers arrested, and if the legions find any churches then they are to be burnt down, the people taken and tortured and killed because he seems to feel quite threatened by this love and peace stuff.

I would have thought that this would be the end of that Christianity – I mean surely all the followers would just drop it and go and find a new, safer religion. But the strange thing is, it isn't stopping people from joining! It may have forced these Christians underground, but they're growing would you believe it! People are just odd sometimes, I guess.

Well, Emperor Diocletian starts demanding that soldiers offer sacrifices directly to him.

George didn't like this and stood up for his faith. I couldn't believe it as, standing before the Emperor himself, the most powerful man in the world, George loudly renounced the Emperor's demand. In front of his fellow soldiers and Tribunes he claimed himself to be a Christian and declared his worship of Jesus Christ.

Diocletian was a bit taken aback, and knowing George to be one of his best men, he attempted to convert George, even offering gifts of land, money and slaves if he made a sacrifice to the Roman gods, but George never accepted: he was clear about this Jesus, so the Emperor had no choice but to have him executed.

Before the execution George gave his wealth to the poor. They killed him after terrible tortures on 23 April 303. I won't go into the details, but believe me, it wasn't nice.

All through it, he kept proclaiming what he believed in. As brave as he had been on the battlefield, he was braver still at the hands of his executioners. I was a bit impressed, I tell you.

We took his body back to Lydda in Palestine for burial, where Christians soon started coming to visit the grave and recognizing him as a martyr: as one prepared to die for what he believed in.

I started asking some of the other lads about this Christian thing, about the bloke they believed in. I'm not sure I'm ready to follow George to martyrdom yet but I can't stop thinking about this Jesus bloke and some of the stories they tell of him. I think I want to know more … I think it's worth the risk.

Activity: Take what you need

In the style of the 'tear-off poster' seen on student noticeboards the world over, why not create some with a bit of scriptural encouragement on them.

On one side arrange the words as above. On the reverse of each tear-off strip put the following verses:

Love	1 John 4.19
Hope	Psalm 119.116
Faith	Luke 7.50
Patience	James 5.8
Courage	Acts 27.25
Understanding	Psalm 119.169
Peace	John 14.27
Passion	Titus 2.12
Healing	Psalm 147.3
Strength	Isaiah 40.29
Beauty	1 Peter 3.4
Freedom	Galatians 5.1

You can put these posters around anywhere, and see what happens. On a Royal Marines base, the 'Courage' went almost immediately. Others quickly followed.

The Royal Marines Prayer[28]

O eternal Lord God, who through many generations has united and inspired the members of our Corps, grant your blessing, we beseech you, on Royal Marines serving all around the Globe. Bestow your crown of righteousness upon all our efforts and endeavours, and may our laurels be those of gallantry and honour, loyalty and courage. We ask these things in the name of him whose courage never failed, our Redeemer, Jesus Christ. Amen.

The elite of fighting forces turns to 'him whose courage never failed, our Redeemer, Jesus Christ'. A powerful thought indeed.

---

28 I am proud to be an Officiating Chaplain to 42 Cdo Royal Marines, Bickleigh.

Application

'But what about the dragon?' someone might ask. The myth most commonly associated with St George is that he fought a hideous dragon and saved a maiden.

The story of George which the Crusaders brought back to England was that of the brave martyr who stood up for his faith: a skilled soldier with compassion and valour. He was adopted as the Patron Saint of England (ousting the properly English St Edmund) in 1349. Illiterate peasants, whose lives of the saints and Bible stories were taught from the gaudy frescoes in medieval churches, knew that George was a soldier and looked to the walls for a saint in armour. They spotted St Michael the Archangel, and recalled his celebrated battle with the dragon from the Revelation to St John the Divine.[29]

It's a short step from that confusion to a medieval romance story about dragons and maidens and Englishmen. Does it matter? Not one bit. The key part of both tales is about standing up to evil (embodied in the form of a dragon) and for what is right: good Christian values worth celebrating.

---

29 Revelation 12.7–9. I always like to make clear that the author of the Revelation is so clearly not the writer of the Gospel nor the letters attributed to the Johannine Community. I wonder why people confuse them: just look at the writing style.

2

Miracles and Revelations

Feeding the Masses: We thought we were going to have to cut those sandwiches very thin ...

Matthew 14.13–21; Mark 6.31–44; Luke 9.10–17; John 6.5–15 but also Mark 8.1–9 and Matthew 15.32–39.

Introduction

Jesus was more than just a good teacher with a cracking set of stories to amuse the people: his ministry was, as John frequently identified, a series of minor revelations or signs which together build into a picture hinting at the power, wonder and awesome nature of God. Through these events which often transcend the laws of physics or rationality and therefore truly exist in that world beyond the describable world – in the realm of God – Christ is able to give us tiny glimpses of a Kingdom beyond our shores and a love beyond all description.

At the feeding of the multitudes, Christ addresses the conflict between physical and spiritual needs and desires, and points to something beyond lunch and towards the new place of encounter with Christ in the most holy sacraments of the altar.

Preparation

Ingredients for bread:

- 1 kg strong bread flour
- 625 ml tepid water
- 30 g fresh yeast, or 3 × 7 g sachets dried yeast
- 2 tablespoons sugar
- 1 level tablespoon fine sea salt
- flour, for dusting

Story

We had been hanging on his every word – the teaching he was giving us just seemed so *real*, so authentic. I could listen to it all day. In fact, we had.

We'd followed him up the mountain, just eager to keep hearing that amazing message. There were loads of us; if I was to take a guess, I'd have said about 4,000 or 5,000, it's so difficult to tell isn't it? No one bothered to make a guest list, but that would have been a reasonable estimate. Whole families, men, women, children, and we were all focused on one thing: the marvellous things he had to tell us. We had no thought for anything else, just get out there and hear what he had to say. We were there the whole day, even though it didn't seem that long, and gradually a small rumble began in the small of my stomach and it grew. None of us had brought any food, it didn't seem necessary at the time, but now, oh what I wouldn't have given for a bite of bread …

I saw his closest disciples talking among themselves. They were obviously worried about the practicalities of feeding all those people. I heard Andy say that he'd found a young lad whose mum had sent him with a picnic – five loaves and two fish – but what would that be with all those people: they were going to have to slice these sandwiches pretty thin.

The Man called the young boy forward and thanked him for his gift, which he seemed happy to share with him. Taking the bread, and then the fish, he raised them to heaven and gave the Father thanks for what little we had. That made me stop and think for a moment – I'm always moaning about what little I have and I usually forget to thank God for the things I do have: human nature maybe, but not always right.

He started to break the bread and the fish into pieces, and he started handing them out to the disciples to give to small groups of us, and he just kept on giving … it went on and on and each of us got much more than we expected: 'Are you sure all this is for me?' I asked Nate and he just shrugged – a gift from God, there was enough to go round.

I ate my fill. I was satisfied. Earlier he'd said that 'man does not live by bread alone but on the word of God'. I'd been filled with bread and fish, but I realized I'd been filled by something much more substantial. Tomorrow, I knew I'd wake physically hungry again – that's life – but my spiritual hunger had been satisfied, the word of God was bountiful, abundant, more than I actually needed … and that marvellous, mysterious man had brought both to me on the mountaintop.

Activity: Make bread!

You can pre-mix the ingredients and then just invite the young people to knead it and lay it out. Small rolls easily double in size and can be cooked in 15 minutes. I have to thank Jamie Oliver for the basis of this recipe.

Ingredients

See the beginning of this section.

Alternatively, if you are using a breadmaker, follow the manufacturer's instructions to produce the dough.

Making Dough

- Pile the flour on to a clean surface and make a large well in the centre. Pour half your water into the well, then add your yeast, sugar and salt and stir with a fork.
- Slowly bring in the flour to the inside of the well. You don't want to break the walls of the well, or the water will go everywhere.
- Continue to bring the flour in to the centre until you get a porridge consistency – then add the remaining water.
- Continue to mix until it's porridgy again, then you can be more aggressive, bringing in all the flour, making the mix less sticky.
- Flour your hands, and pat and push the dough together with all the remaining flour.

Kneading

- This is where young people like to get stuck in! With a bit of elbow grease, simply push, fold, slap and roll the dough around, over and over, for four or five minutes until you have a silky and elastic dough. You might want to recall Scriptures about God forming and shaping us.
- Flour the top of your dough. Put it in a bowl, cover with cling-film, and allow it to prove for about half an hour until doubled in size – ideally in a warm, moist, draught-free place. This will improve the flavour and texture of your dough. Waiting is a key part of it: nothing worthwhile ever happens immediately, and, like the work of the Holy Spirit, growth happens in quiet, often unseen ways.
- Once the dough has doubled in size, knock the air out for 30 seconds by bashing it and squashing it. You can now shape it or flavour it as required and leave it to prove for a second time for 30 minutes to an hour until it has doubled in size once more. This is the most important part, as the second prove will give it the air that finally ends up being cooked into your bread, giving you the really light, soft texture that we all love in fresh bread.
- Preheat the oven to 180°C/350°F/gas 4. Very gently place your bread dough on to a flour-dusted baking tray and into the preheated oven.
- Jamie says you must not slam the oven door or you'll lose the air that you need for that light, airy, Holy Spirit-filled effect.
- Bake for 25–30 minutes or until cooked and golden brown. You can tell if it's cooked by tapping its bottom – if it sounds hollow, it's done, if it doesn't then pop it back in for a little longer.
- Once cooked, place on a rack and allow it to cool for at least 30 minutes.
- It is best shared. You could even celebrate the Eucharist with it!

Remember Psalm 34.8: 'Taste and see that the Lord is good!'

The Wedding at Cana: Party on!

John 2.1–11.

Introduction

I really fail to understand why some should take such a dim view of the created world, and see it all as sin, corruption, evil. The Old Testament writers knew that God's blessings were manifest in his creation, and oil and wine were literal, visceral reminders of those blessings. When the psalmist wrote of 'wine that gladdens the heart'[30] it was supposed to be a good thing, a celebration. To regard it as the essence of so much evil that you avoid it even in your worship must appear strange to the God who made all creation 'and saw that it was good'.[31]

Jesus had a very different take on the matter: the Last Supper did not feature unfermented grape juice. His celebration of all creation and love of life earned him criticism as 'a glutton and a drunkard' as they looked beyond the restrictive kosher diet laws and towards a full engagement with all that God made. Although the Jewish laws were packed with all kinds of prohibitions and 'thou shalt nots', God is not about putting a brake on life, but rather enabling us to live it powerfully, as is the will of God.

I don't understand why people should think that the Church should stand in the way, constantly say 'No', disapprove and seem like a bunch of killjoys, when Jesus said, 'I came that you may have life, life in all its fullness' (John 10.10).

The faith is about living life to the full, respecting God, respecting others. How can you therefore turn down that second glass of wine I'm offering you?

Preparation

You can illustrate this story very well by having a glass jug filled with water and a drinking glass. In the bottom of the glass you can put some food col-

---

30 Psalm 104.15.
31 Genesis 1.31.

ouring (which works better than blackcurrant juice). I sometimes hide the bottom of the glass with a strip of masking tape and hold it with my hand around the bottom so they can't see it. As you describe pouring out the wine, tip the water into the glass and instant wine!

For the mocktails, gather some cocktail shakers, paper umbrellas, stirrers and a mixture of cocktail glasses. You can obtain plastic ones from the bargain shops if you don't want to risk glass. You will also need ice, lemons and a variety of fruit juices and soft drinks to taste. Some examples are given below.

Story

We all love a wedding, don't we? An uninhibited party. Back in the day, the wedding celebration wasn't a single evening, it lasted for days. The wine flowed, the dancing was fantastic, the food was plentiful and the atmosphere was … atmospheric!

Working a celebration like that, as a wine waiter like I was, was hard work, I mean the whole village was invited, relatives from all over the place, the place was packed!

Some of the guests can get a bit lairy once the wine has flowed a bit, so I always keep an eye on the wine stocks because if we were to run out with the party in full swing, well there'd be a riot! It would reflect badly on the groom as well, damage his reputation in the eyes of all in the village.

Well, as I said, it was a rocking party – and the revellers were drinking well. I noticed that we were getting to the bottom of the barrel, as it were. One of the ladies in the group noticed me looking a little worried. She leaned over, and without fuss she just smiled at me: 'I'll get it sorted.' I had no idea how she was going to replenish the wine. I wondered if she kept a few bottles back at home, but that wouldn't last any time at all.

She got up and went to talk to a big burly bloke. He looked a bit like her, I suppose. He treated her with some respect, and I clicked that it was her son she was talking to. As I continued my work clearing the tables, I passed by as they were talking.

'They're running out of wine.'

'It's not my time yet, Mum …'

'Can't you do anything?' And with that she tapped me on the arm as I passed. 'This is my son – do as he says.'

The son walked with me to the back of the hall, where we kept the washing containers – huge barrels of water for the ritual washing we undertake as part of our faith. Seven barrels, gallons and gallons of water. No wine back here though …

He told me and the other waiters to fill our wine jugs from the washing barrels. Was he mad? We all knew it was just water in those barrels. We had filled them ourselves but, shrugging, we did so – well you see, he was a big lad and I thought I'd humour him a bit in case he got a bit rough. *(You can fill your wine glass at this point.)*

As I turned the tap to pour out the water, I had the shock of my life. It wasn't water! Deepest, dark red, and with an aroma that filled the room. It was wine, good wine. I couldn't resist a taste, after all we had been working hard and so a quick glass wouldn't hurt … *(Taking a sip lends authenticity to your storytelling.)* And it was good. It was better than good. It was amazing wine.

I called over the head waiter. He had to see this. Each one of these seven massive barrels was filled with this amazing wine. He tasted. He smacked his lips. He nodded. He smiled.

He then clicked his fingers and got us out serving, and the party continued to rock. Most people put out the good wine first, and then when everyone is a little less fussy, out comes the cheap wine, but no. Today the party featured the best at the last. No one in the bridal parties knew where this wine had come from: just us workers.

The taste: oh it was so sweet, so good. Like a taste of heaven. I remembered that the old Rabbi used to teach us the words of the psalm, 'taste and see that the Lord is good',[32] and that man somehow made those words real. As I tasted that wonderful wine, I thought I had tasted what paradise would be like. I saw him smiling at me a little later, and it was almost as though he knew that I had got it, made that connection; and it seemed to please him.

Activity: Mocktails[33]

If we are going to play with the idea of Psalm 34.8 and 'taste and see that the Lord is good' then we should be prepared for some multisensory experience, without the need for alcohol. Don't get me wrong: we should not shun alcohol as the work of the devil (for as we have seen, Scripture and our Lord clearly take a different view) but should encourage moderation, sense and balance for adulthood, not promote underage drinking!

There is so much fun to be had with the mixing of non-alcoholic cocktails or 'mocktails' as they are often called. Fruit juices and soft drinks are the basis of many adult cocktails and so through these we can enjoy the taste sensations of God's creations without alcohol.

---

32 Psalm 34.8.

33 Adapted with grateful thanks and after some fun experimentation from the NetMums site: http://www.netmums.com/family-food/party-food/non-alcoholic-cocktails

You can dress up the whole event with tuxedos and ballgowns and make a real 'James Bond – ooHeaven' theme to it.[34] The paraphernalia of cocktails are part of the fun as well: fancy glasses, paper umbrellas and cocktail shakers. Some of these recipes need blending to make them smooth. Give everyone the chance to mix and shake their own cocktails, starting with a couple of these classic mocktails and then encouraging them to experiment to create a new recipe!

The following recipes use a shot glass to ensure a consistent measure. You can scale up the volumes according to how many want to share.

- **Acapulco Gold:** Shake together six shots of pineapple juice, one shot of grapefruit juice, two tablespoons of coconut cream, two tablespoons of fresh cream and a scoop of crushed ice. Serve unstrained.
- **Atomic Cat:** Add 4 oz of orange juice and 4 oz of tonic water to a long glass and fill with crushed ice.
- **Banana Smoothie:** Put one banana, a pinch of nutmeg, half a teaspoon of vanilla extract, a cup of milk and two cups of crushed ice in a blender and whip into a thick smoothie.
- **Berry Surprise:** Blend one cup of strawberries, a cup of pineapple chunks, half a cup of raspberries and a splash of lime cordial together and serve over ice.
- **California Smoothie:** Place seven large strawberries in a container and freeze for an hour. Put 8 oz lemon yogurt, half a cup of orange juice and the frozen strawberries in a blender and mix until smooth. Add ice and chopped strawberries to garnish.
- **Capucine:** Shake a shot of peppermint cordial and four shots of cream in a cocktail shaker, add crushed ice and decorate with grated chocolate.
- **Cinderella:** Mix two shots of pineapple juice, orange juice and lemon juice in a shaker, add ice, soda water and a dash of grenadine to give it a lovely berry colour. Garnish with a slice of pineapple or a cherry.
- **Fruitburst:** Blend an apple, three carrots and a mango until smooth, then add seven shots of freshly squeezed oranges and six strawberries and blend on a low speed. Sieve and serve over ice.
- **Grapefruit Ice Cream Soda:** Add two tablespoons of grapefruit juice to a glass with a small pinch of sugar and stir until the sugar has thoroughly

---

34 2013 National Youth Pilgrimage to the Shrine of Our Lady of Walsingham.

dissolved. Top up with soda water and a generous spoonful of vanilla ice cream.

- **Grapefruit Mojito:** Put some fresh mint leaves in the bottom of a glass and then add a generous amount of crushed ice. Stir two tablespoons of grapefruit juice with a quarter teaspoon of honey until the honey is entirely dissolved. Transfer the dissolved honey/grapefruit juice to the cocktail shaker with four additional tablespoons of grapefruit juice and give it a good shake with ice. Strain into a tumbler glass and serve.
- **Jungle Juice:** Place a banana, four tablespoons of orange juice and a dash of ginger ale in a blender and whizz on a medium speed until liquefied. Pour into a glass over ice.
- **Lemon Daisy:** Put a shot of lemon juice and a large dash of grenadine into a glass, stir together and add ice. Top the glass with half lemonade and half soda for a fizzy, fruity extravaganza.
- **Mickey Mouse:** Add 3 oz tomato juice, a dash of lemon juice, half a teaspoon of Worcestershire sauce and three drops of Tabasco in a cocktail shaker and fuse together. Pour into a glass over ice and add a lime wedge on the side.
- **Morning Star:** Put a teaspoon of honey, half a teaspoon of sugar, three pineapple chunks, ten shots of pineapple juice and a cup of mineral water in a blender and whizz until smooth.
- **Orangatang:** Mix half orange juice and half cranberry juice in a shaker. Serve with a straw and crushed ice.
- **Passion Fruit Spritzer:** Pour 4 oz of passion fruit juice into a flute glass and top with soda and a lime wedge.
- **Peach Smoothie:** Put 15 oz sliced peaches, four scoops of vanilla ice cream, half a cup of orange juice and a small dash of milk in a blender and whizz until soft.
- **Pomegranate Ice:** Pile lots of cracked ice high in a glass and add four shots of grenadine. Serve with a straw.
- **Rainbow Punch:** Put three tablespoons of orange juice, three tablespoons of grapefruit juice, a dash of grenadine and a tablespoon of lime juice into a cocktail shaker and shake the juices together. Strain into a glass and top up with soda water for a fruity, colourful concoction.
- **Scarlet Lady:** Blend 4 oz of watermelon and five red grapes in a food processor until smooth, then add three shots of grapefruit juice and re-blend until smooth. Strain into a glass with chopped grapes to decorate.

- **Seabreeze:** Shake four shots of cranberry juice and two shots of grapefruit juice with ice and pour into a tumbler.
- **Strawberry Lemonade:** Throw a shot of lemon juice, a pinch of sugar, ten strawberries and a cup of water into a blender and mix until smooth.
- **Tangerine Dream:** Shake three shots of grapefruit juice, three shots of orange juice and two shots of lemon juice, pour in a glass and fill with ice cubes.
- **Toothless Shark:** Pour half a tablespoon of grenadine into a long glass and separately blend six tablespoons of orange juice with half a tablespoon of lime juice. Carefully pour the orange and lime juice into the glass for a colourful layered effect.
- **Ugly Bug:** Mix three tablespoons of grapefruit juice, pineapple juice, orange juice and prune juice together in a glass and chill in the fridge until deliciously cool.
- **Vanilla Banana Smoothie:** Put two chopped bananas and a cup of vanilla ice cream in a blender, add half a teaspoon of vanilla extract, a cup of milk and half a cup of fresh orange juice. Mix until thick and smooth.

Application

God's gifts, God's blessings to us are never just like little drops: never just enough to get by, but more than enough. At that wedding, a couple of bottles would have been fine. Yet God had different plans. His bounteous goodness is more than we can ever need: barrels and barrels of the stuff!

In many ways the story of the wedding tells us much about the way in which God works. In much the same way as wine is created in the dark, with the hidden action of yeast to transform simple grape juice into tasty wine, so God's Holy Spirit works quietly, often hidden, in order to transform us from the ordinary into the extraordinary. We have to be open to the work of the yeast (Jesus himself spoke about the work of yeast in bread, giving life, air and taste), of the Spirit in our lives and to trust in its transforming work.

Walking on Water: You can't always make it on your own

Matthew 14.22–33.

Introduction

We love to feel independent, capable, in control. Few of us are. The more important step in your faith journey is to realize that you can't always make it on your own. No one can tell you that: you have to work it out for yourself.

Preparation

Equipment

- A CD player, or a laptop and a copy of U2's 'Sometimes you can't make it on your own'.
- Large ikons of Christ: images of the *Pantocrator* are best, printed out and perhaps laminated to make them rigid.
- Mirror tiles.
- Some strong ('gaffer') tape.

Join the mirrors and the ikons as below:

Ikon of Christ — — Mirror

Tape to connect

Story

Some of our little group were fishermen: experienced sailors who knew the wind and the waves, how to avoid the rocks just below the surface and steer around the ship-wrecks that littered this lake which formed the centre of our lives and our livelihoods: the lake or the sea of Galilee.

We were piloting the boat from one side to the other and then I looked out over the water and saw something on the surface, not swimming, but actually *on* the water. It was more than just a something, it was a someone, no more than just an anyone …

We were terrified, well you would be wouldn't you? And while he was still some way off from us, he called out 'Don't be afraid'; no of course not, we're quite used to seeing people walking on water around here. We were a long way out to sea, there was clearly no shallow bit, or a platform underneath, he … was … actually … doing … it!

Peter saw who it was – he might not have been the brightest among us, but he was certainly the quickest on the uptake: it was him!

'Come and join me,' he said. Peter was unflinching, if Jesus said that it was okay then it was fine. So, he put one foot over the side. Any other time I saw him do that, things were about to get wet, but … he looked even more confident.

'Yes, that's right,' Jesus encouraged him, and so Peter put his other foot over and onto the water. That's right, I couldn't believe it myself, onto not into the water.

Slowly, tentatively, carefully even, Peter started over towards where Jesus was, hands on hips, grinning broadly.

He was making good progress, and then I think his overconfidence did for him. Maybe he thought he was doing so well, and how clever he was, because I saw his excited smile vanish, and he started to lose it, the panic came into his eyes and he started to slide into the deep water.

Just before he went under, suddenly Jesus was by his side, had his hand, pulled him up and had him in a moment back, safe in the boat. Peter looked a bit sheepish. He should have known that he couldn't do this on his own, that it was through him that he was able to do amazing things.

Activity: Reflect

Encourage people to place themself in front of the ikon and the mirror so that they are able to see both themself and the ikon.

As the music plays, so the participant can reflect on the face of Christ and seek, as St Francis prayed that others might see, the face of Christ in us.

Application

How often when something goes wrong in our lives do we blame it on others, on God, 'Why does God punish me like this?' and yet how often when things go right do we claim it is through our own skill and artistry, and never give God a second thought in it?

The Daughter Who Was Dead

Mark 5.21–43; Matthew 9.18–26; Luke 8.40–45.

Introduction

My own personal experience of the power of God's healing is not one of miraculous events: of people jumping up and picking up their bed and walking away, or throwing aside their crutches. The healing power of God comes in many forms, and while on occasion it may be for some instant and miraculous, often it comes about slowly and often through the agency of others.

The wise priest who laid hands upon me and anointed me with the oil of healing prior to my eye surgery reminded me that God created the laser beams – and the hands that wielded them. God created the chemotherapy and the surgeon and the insulin and guided those who discovered it. There is not a stark choice between medical science and faith, but healing takes both.

Sometimes, we should accept that God's healing might also be found in the departure from this life. Death is not the end, but a waypoint and a journey to be with God once again, where every tear shall be wiped away and all things will be restored to fullness.[35]

---

35 Revelation 21.4.

Preparation

No equipment is required, but I strongly recommend a period of prayer among the team before offering prayers for healing. You are the conduit for God's healing, and that requires openness to his grace.

Come, Holy Spirit,
fill the hearts of your faithful people,
and kindle in them the fire of your love.
May this space become a place of encounter with you,
A place of healing, a place of renewal.
May we become your instruments of grace
and signs of your love to those who are entrusted to us.
Work through us and with us
so that all to whom we minister are
granted a glimpse of your unfailing power,
in the name of Christ, our Saviour, Redeemer and Healer.
Amen.

Story

My daughter, my daughter – so sick, so weak. I am truly afraid that she is nearing the end. She has been ill for so long and although we've always managed to get her through it, I'm not sure how long she will last. She struggles for breath with the smallest exertion, and there is no colour in her – she looks pale, blue even. I don't think there is much more heart in her any more.

I heard that he was in our town, moving through on his teaching and healing tour. I'd heard so many good things about what he had to say, but also some of the other rumours about him: that he'd been thrown out of the Samaritan towns for killing a whole herd of pigs – something to do with an exorcism and a big cliff – for defying the authorities and undermining the synagogue by continually bringing up this 'God loves you' stuff, as if you ought to be telling people that.

When he came to the synagogue, *my* synagogue, I just had to ask him. Urgently, I approached him, with maybe even a hint of desperation in my voice, 'Please, teacher, come and be with my daughter, I fear she may die …'

He looked at me, and raised an eyebrow. I felt as though he could sense my very innermost fears, my anxiety; and suddenly my position as one of the great and the good of this synagogue didn't seem important any more; my social standing was worthless, all that mattered was the daughter whom I loved with all my heart.

'Yes, Jairus, let us go ...'

Getting him out and away from the crowd clamouring for him wasn't going to be easy: they were pressing in on him from every side, reaching for him, anxious to touch him.

The worst possible thing happened. He was delayed. Some woman touched him and he stopped to deal with her.[36] She was one of those dirty, unclean women, and all the while he was spending with her my beautiful, pure daughter was slipping away. As he finished blessing and sending that old woman away, one of my staff came up. He looked crestfallen, depressed. I knew what it meant. The end.

I turned to him and shrugged. No point in bothering him now.

He didn't seem bothered. 'Oh, I am sure she will be fine. Let's go.'

And that was it. He walked out of the synagogue, heading to my house, leaving me stranded with just those few words of his. Desolated. I supposed that he was going on to join the mourners: to do his duty by the bedside and to join his tears with ours.

I trudged back to my house with a heavy heart. As I turned the corner I was expecting to hear the crying of the household, the lamenting, the sound of loss and pain. But I couldn't hear it. Inside I was all chewed up with the loss, and thought that to hear others in such mourning would help me pour it out, but I couldn't hear it.

Instead, there was laughter. Laughter? Laughter at a time like this! I was so angry – the disrespect! I was ready to punch the first person I met, and so I rushed towards where my lovely, dead and now unlamented daughter lay. As I rushed up the stairs, I heard more laughter, but also a familiar sound, a special sound, a sound that I loved to hear: *her* laughter.

As I entered the room, my grief and my anger melted away to see my wonderful daughter sat up on the edge of the bed, flushed with life, filled with joy and surrounded by my wife and friends, It was a ... a miracle!

'The Master just came in, took her by the hand and said, "Come on, little one, get up" ... and she did. She just ... got ... up!' my wife exclaimed. 'She was dead, but he just said she was sleeping.'

With a word he raised her from the sleep of death to life again. We embraced, all three of us.

She was fine. Just like he said. Yes, it would be fine. How could I have doubted?

---

36 See *Uncomfortable Realities: The Woman Who Bled*, p. 15.

Activity: Praying for healing

Whether people seek healing for themselves or on behalf of others, prayer for healing can be a powerful thing. It seldom happens dramatically, and yet in quiet, almost hidden ways, God's healing can bring comfort, peace, restoration and occasionally a good death. The latter is not always a failure of prayer, but the fulfilment of it.

The use of oil in healing prayers is profoundly scriptural. The letter of James says:

> Is anyone among you ill? Let them call the priests of the church to pray over them and anoint them with oil in the name of the Lord. And the prayer offered in faith will make the sick person well; the Lord will raise them up. If they have sinned, they will be forgiven.

> James 5.14–15

Some prayers for healing can involve the imposition of hands on the head. If the group are receptive and prayerful, this can be done one to another. It should never be done when a leader is alone with young people to ensure adequate safeguarding.

The Holy Oil, consecrated by a bishop on Maundy Thursday, is an outward sign of the sacrament of healing and is usually administered by a priest.

Laying on of hands and anointing

Hands are laid on the head, in silence, then the forehead is marked with the sign of the cross with the Oil of Healing.

Through this holy anointing
may the Lord in his love and mercy
help you with the grace of the Holy Spirit.

The palms of the hands are anointed with a cross on each palm.

May the Lord who frees you from sin save you and raise you up.

After annointing.

Let us pray.

Father in heaven,
through this holy anointing
grant our brothers and sisters comfort in their suffering.
When they are afraid, give them courage;
when afflicted, give them patience;
when dejected, afford them hope;
and when alone, assure them of the support of your holy people.
We ask this in the name of Jesus, the Lord.
Amen.

Application

Young people, for whom life is a vast expanse and for whom death is almost as inconceivable as middle age, may have many questions about death and loss. They may have experienced the loss of a relative or more significantly they may be fearful of that event. I always want to emphasize that death is a part of life, and after death our relationship with the departed has not ended, but has changed: memories, love and prayer enable us to continue the bond with someone and we each take a little bit of that person with us to the end of our own lives.

A hundred or so years ago, the Victorians were obsessed with death: dressing in black, long periods of mourning and Gothic novels, and were afraid to speak of sex. Today's society is obsessed with sex and afraid to speak of death. You cannot avoid death with silence. The Christian hope is concerned with life *through* death and Christ shows us the way: we can point to the resurrected Christ and see the promise made to us. This is not an empty promise of 'jam tomorrow' but a sure hope that there is more to life than this.

Healing of the Outcasts

Luke 17.11–19.

Introduction

So often we seek to marginalize others. Young people who seek peer approval above all things seek to run with the pack, identify themselves with like-minded others and even when dressing to stand out, do so to be 'one of the group'. It takes courage to move in a different direction or to dance to a different beat.

Preparation

No equipment is required.

Story

I don't like lepers. There. I said it.

When I say leprosy, it's not necessarily the Hansen's disease that we know as leprosy today. Back in the day, it was a sort of catch-all phrase for all sorts of skin disease. However, whether it meant your limbs losing sensitivity, getting damaged and rotting because there isn't *any* treatment available or just a bit of a nasty rash, to us it's all leprosy. That's bad news, because it simply cuts you off from society: exiled from your home and family, sent into the desert. No hope of work, no hope of improvement, just begging and starvation to look forward to. The very thought of leprosy sends a shiver down my spine. And seeing a leper on the road? No, you have to avoid them, cross the road, stay well away from them.

Travelling down the road we came across a whole group of them: a band of ten in various stages of disfigurement. All of us wanted to just get away from that area, as though even being within the same county as them would be contagious. But not him. Oh no, of course not him. He strides over to them, lying pathetically at the side of the road, crying for charity.

One of them recognizes Jesus and they all start begging, not for money but for healing. They have heard he can do amazing things and they naturally want a part of it. Although just being here makes me feel really jumpy, I can't help but notice that Jesus is so comfortable, so caring, so interested in them, not just as diseased bodies, but as *people*.

'Go and show yourselves to the priests, go and get a certificate which proves you're okay now,' he said to them.

We looked at each other a bit puzzled. He hadn't done anything to them, for them, and yet he was treating them as though they were already healed! The ten men picked themselves up and headed towards the city. Still a bit confused, we went on our way following Jesus in the opposite direction.

A short time later, someone comes up behind us, panting. He has run to catch us up. It is one of the lepers, or should I say now, ex-lepers because he looks … so different! He falls at Jesus' feet and thanks him with real sincerity. As they were walking back to the city, they were healed. The rest decided to keep on going and get the bill of health. But he just knew he had to get back and thank Jesus, the paperwork could wait. You can tell from his accent that he isn't from around here, probably not even one of us.

Jesus smiles that wry smile of his, and asks the man gently, 'Where are the others?' He turns to us: 'I thought God had healed all ten, but only this man, a Samaritan at that' (I knew he wasn't a proper local!) 'comes back.' He doesn't sound disappointed, even though I would – just resigned.

'Go in peace,' he tells the man and sends him on his way. Even the thanks of just one of the ten seems to make him happy.

Prayer: No one left behind

Gather the group around in a circle. If they are comfortable, they can hold on to the next person's shoulder, or put their hands into the middle, like the spokes of a wheel.

There are no gaps in this circle, because our circle is complete. We are linked one to another, as children of God, as brothers and sisters in Christ. All are invited to be a part of this chain, all are welcome, all are valued, each as important as the next.

No one gets left behind, no one can go amiss. The good shepherd will search for the lost and the wayward and draw them back into this fold. Your invitation to this never-ending circle will always be there.

When we scatter, we are still connected, when we are assailed, we stand together; when we are lost, we can find each other, for we are connected by Christ the thread woven between us. Amen.

3

God's Saving Acts

Jonah: Running away never achieved anything

Introduction

God asks amazing things of us. Often they are scary or challenging and definitely out of our comfort zone. In fact, if you are trying to work out what God is asking of you, you can always guarantee that the option he really wants is the toughest option. Through that, he makes great things happen. The problem is, we have to trust him.

Preparation

No equipment is required. When leading the liturgy, the person interrupting the prayers has to manage the careful balance between preventing people from just blindly saying the prayer and losing the gentle, yet challenging tone.

Slam Poem:[37] *Running away never achieved anything*

God had a plan,
a plan for the man.
The man they all called Jonah.

Jonah was the man,
and part of the plan
was to go to the town they called Ninevah!

Tell all the guys
to go back on their lies
and turn back to God to live justly.

But Jonah said 'No way!'
and he chose to run away
'It's too much of a task for anyone.'

He tried to escape,
go for the break.
Jump on a ship and head outa here.

But you can't stop the Man
when he has a plan.
He'll catch up with you anyways.

The storm it did blow,
the sailors below
sensed it was all of Jonah's making.

And so the crew
overboard Jonah threw
and into the briny sea they left him.

---

37 Cooler than rap, looser than a normal poem, slam poems are characterized by a greater emphasis on rhythm than rhyme; although admittedly this slam poem holds to a tighter rhythmic scheme than many slam poems. The best slam poet in the world is, I believe, Harry Baker. See http://www.facebook.com/harrybakerpoetry

In the middle of the gale
he was swallowed by a whale,
Could anything worse have happened to him?

Three days and three nights
he sheltered in the side
of the fish that had consumed him.

It was dark, it was dank,
goodness me, it stank!
But in there Jonah changed his mind.

Then the fish did a vomit
and quicker than a comet
Jonah found himself back on the shore.

He had to follow through the plan,
the plan of the Man
to bring Ninevah back to Jehovah.

So he walked into town
declaring what was going down
and what they had to do to get righteous.

The people all heard
Jonah's terrifying word
and the prophecy he was bringing forward.

So they all sat down
and took on the frown
of people who knew they were sorry.

God saw they had changed,
wouldn't do it again,
Knew they had come back to him.

God was the Master
so averted the disaster
and promised that it wouldn't happen.

Jonah had a task
but when he was asked
he thought he wasn't up to it.

But God really knew
what Jonah could do
which is the reason why God chose him.

So if he asks you to do
something scary or new
don't hesitate or try to avoid it.

Because God has a plan
and you are the man
or the woman he wants to achieve it!

So don't be afraid
or try to run away
and make sure
you avoid any boat trips!

Liturgy: The Lord's Prayer Challenge

One person leads the group in the Lord's Prayer,[38] while another (in italics here) keeps challenging the words. It is difficult to interrupt effectively, but it makes each petition of this oft-repeated-without-thought prayer extremely powerful and challenging.

Our Father in heaven
Don't say 'Father' if you do not behave like a son or daughter.
Don't say 'Our' if you only think of yourself.

Hallowed be your name
Don't say 'Hallowed' if you do not honour that name.

---

38 Based on an original idea by Capt. Gordon Banks CA, to whom many thanks are due for his creativity and inspiration.

Your Kingdom come
Don't say 'Your Kingdom come' if you are weighed down with material goods.

Your will be done, On earth as in heaven
Don't say 'Thy will be done' if you do not accept the hard bits.
Don't say 'as in heaven' if you only think about earthly matters.

Give us this day our daily bread
Don't say 'Our daily bread' if you have no concern for the hungry or the homeless.

Forgive us our sins, as we forgive those who sin against us
Don't say 'Forgive us our sins' if you remain angry with someone.

Lead us not into temptation
Don't say 'Lead us not into temptation' if you intend to continue sinning.

But deliver us from evil
Don't say 'Deliver us from evil' if you are not willing to make a stand against injustice.

For the Kingdom, the Power and the Glory are yours, now and for ever. Amen.
Don't say 'AMEN' without considering the words of your prayer!

Application

Think about things in our past that we have tried to run away from. It may be something small, something we encounter often and now try to avoid or it could be just one big enormous, apparently insurmountable thing. We should perhaps ask ourselves, 'Will running away solve the problem? What is it that is so scary?'

I want to suggest that the main fear is not so much the task in hand, but the fear of the unknown and the sense that we don't have the resources inside us to achieve what we believe is being asked of us.

Of course we can't. Few things can be achieved without God's help. We just need to be brave enough to realize it. To be built up by God, we need to be stripped away, and sometimes the masks that we hide behind are the insecurities which prevent us from being truly open to God. By surrendering to God, we lay ourselves open to his possibilities rather than our own. Most of my failings have been when I have failed to trust in him. If I let *his will be done* then it always seems to work out, not always as I expected, but far more than I could have imagined.

St Augustine: Where prayer makes all the difference

Introduction

We often think of saints as unbelievably holy people: beyond the rest of us and amazingly pious. I am sure they are really more like us all. To be aware of God is the beginning of wisdom[39] and the gift of sainthood is really in recognition of their relationship with God which led them to do marvellous things in his name. None were more aware of their need of God than a headstrong and clever young man from North Africa.

Preparation

No equipment is required.

Story

Gus was always a bit of a handful for his mum. He was keenly intelligent, clearly. He knew all the answers, and they didn't seem to match up with what he heard from the family at home. As a result, he went a bit off the rails: got a girl in trouble, if you know what I mean, got involved in one of those dodgy religious cults and finally ran off to

---

39 Better than 'fear' don't you think? Psalm 111.10.

live a bit of a party-life in a foreign country where he went to study: a big town in Italy called Milan.

His mum, however, never lost faith in him. She kept on praying for him. She kept the faith for him, even if he didn't have any space for faith in his life. Prayer: just plugging away, and knowing that God would sort it all out.

On the continent, Gus was to meet an amazing man, a holy man. Bosie was a bishop, of all things! He'd been chosen in a rather bizarre way, but rather than being the laughing-stock of the Church, Bosie became really, really good at it. He was also devastatingly clever, amazingly faithful and had a good line of argument, so when cocky young Gus meets him, Bosie has some good answers. Gus and Bosie spend some time in the intellectual cut and thrust.

And God sorts it all out. Gus's mum, Monica, keeps on with the prayer for him, and through his encounter with Bosie, Gus develops a faith. This is a powerful faith, a deep and inspiring faith and so unlike the shallow stuff he'd dabbled with before.

Gus later himself becomes a priest and then a bishop, back home in his homeland of North Africa. His writing changed the look and feel and intellectual rigour of the whole Church, and for that he was made a saint: St Augustine of Hippo.[40]

St Augustine's *Confessions*, which is effectively one of the earliest autobiographies around, is a powerful reflection on his own dissolute life and God's grace and goodness. It shows that many Christians come to faith after a somewhat *colourful* life and that we become the Christians and the human beings we are because of, not in spite of, what we have done in the past.

For her faith and trust, his mum was also made a saint: St Monica. Proper proof if it were ever needed that faithful prayer – eventually – pays off.

Application

In this story, I have modernized the names: St Augustine becomes Gus; St Ambrose, Bishop of Milan, becomes Bosie.

There are still so many people in this world who consider themselves beyond redemption: beyond God's help. It's understandable because I suspect it's a position many of us have been in. The experience of grace, undeserved forgiveness freely given, is hard to accept, but an essential part of the experience of faith. It doesn't come in a flash, but needs to dawn slowly upon us, like the

---

40 It is a real place in North Africa, I promise you.

daybreak. Even if our acceptance of Christ comes as an epiphanous moment, the reality of grace can (and perhaps should) be a slower development.

However, to continue to resist the grace of God is really a sinful act: the sin of pride – to believe yourself so bad that you are beyond help – is a conceit of the highest vanity. Christ did not go to the cross for some, but for the world.

4

The Spread of the Good News

The Beatitudes

Matthew 5.3–12.

Introduction

The collected name for this, Christ's most powerful teaching distilled into a few pithy statements, is 'Beatitudes' which is derived from the Latin word for 'Blessed'. Some translations read this as 'Happy', but this is a woefully poor translation. Although to be blessed by God is to be happy, it transcends merely feeling good into a deeper engagement with the divine. I feel sometimes that there simply aren't enough blessings in the world, and we should action blessings to all those around us in both what we do and what we say. Although the sacramental act of blessing remains the function of a priest, the calling of God's blessing upon all is the work of all Christians.

Even as a lay person, you should always have the words of Aaron to hand to finish a meeting, an assembly or a session:[41]

May the Lord bless you, and keep you.
May the Lord make his face to shine upon you.
May the Lord be gracious to you, and give you his peace.

---

41 Numbers 6.24–26.

And may the blessing of + Father, Son and Holy Spirit be upon us all, this [day/night] and always. Amen.

Some, in the process of denying the divinity of the Lord, might say, 'Oh well, Jesus was a great moral teacher' and point to this as an example, but the ethical values which Christ teaches are not secular values but the values of God. You cannot exercise Christ's ethical teaching without engaging in God ... because he *is* God.

Preparation

Equipment: A pile of recent newspapers, scissors and glue, or internet access.

Story

Of all the things he taught us, I will never forget when he summed it all up on that mountain top. We gathered at his feet and he said:

Blessed are those who know they need God in their lives, who realize that going it alone is just vanity and that relying on your own strength, skill or wit will only take you so far. God will respond to all those who respond to him with the ultimate prize.

Blessed are those who are aware of their shortcomings, and don't cover them up with a bit of a swagger or an 'Am I bovvered?' attitude. Blessed are those who aren't afraid to recognize that we choose our own way more often than we choose God's and fall into sin. Blessed rather are those who realize there are things to sort out in their lives, for God will help them find true inner peace.

Blessed are those who don't seek power or money or influence for themselves, but seek to build God's Kingdom in this world, for they will see their dreams of equality and justice for all prevail when God's love is known throughout the world.

Blessed are those who are so desperate for justice, mercy and fairness that it feels like ravening hunger: God will satisfy them.

Blessed are those who are willing to show mercy, love and forgiveness to others, even those who hurt them. God will respond to them with even more mercy, love and forgiveness.

Blessed are those who seek to live pure and holy lives, following God's teachings and seeking to welcome the outcast, the stranger, the poor, the addicted and the desperate, for as they look into their eyes with care and compassion they will see the face of God.

Blessed are those who seek peace over war, unity over division, agreement over disagreement, prayer over condemnation: these are the ways in which we draw close to the heart of God. God hates …? God hates no one. Ever.

Blessed are those who are given a hard time for standing up for what is right, what is truly of God even in the face of the state, the establishment, society, those who claim to know better than you, your so-called friends. Blessed are those who are imprisoned or killed for showing God's love. The ultimate prize is theirs.

God will bless you when people laugh at you or make all kinds of 'rational' scientific arguments against your intelligence on Twitter because you follow me, even though it's not a black and white, either/or kind of argument. Some will be thrown into prison for standing up against evil in the world. Never lose heart, even though it's a tough call, because great is God's reward for you in this world and the next.

You are not the first, and you won't be the last. Keep on.

Activity: Newspaper scan

A trawl through local and national newspapers across the spectrum of class and quality can identify news stories which conform to either the values of the world or the values of God. Scissors and glue can create a collage of words and images which highlight these contrasts: inner beauty against the vacuous concept of beauty, eating disorders pushed at young women, the nihilism of the music industry and the greed and corruption of 'business' which pervades our papers daily.

This can be done online as well. The Evernote[42] Webclipper application enables you to select all or part of a webpage and save it in the popular free multiplatform notetaking software so it can be compiled into a new 'newspaper' or webpage which does much the same without further endangering the supply of fish wrappers.

Application

That which the world values – money, power, influence, sex, more, more, more – is so far from that which God values: love, joy, peace, patience, kindness, goodness, faithfulness, gentleness, self-control.[43]

Young people have always been keen to swim against the tide: to be countercultural, revolutionary, different. I tell young people that the only way to be totally radical is to be a Christian. While others clamour after labels and how many Facebook friends they have, the last truly countercultural act is to follow Christ.

As I retold the teaching of the Beatitudes, I showed on screen a sloweddown video of the man who stood in front of the tanks in Tiananmen Square:

or this link: http://bit.ly/WpR1mK

It seems to say so much about the values of the Beatitudes against the forces of evil. Young people may not have even been born when the students were crushed in the Square, but they can identify with the image, and more significantly the ideas that the image evokes.

---

42 http://www.evernote.com/
43 Galatians 5.22–23.

Emmaus: A long walk to freedom

Luke 24.13–35.

Introduction

'The Lord is here' we say at the gathering around the holy table. No celebration of the Eucharist happens without the expectation of the Lord turning up. In the beginning though, it was much more unexpected.

Preparation

You will need a large sheet of polythene or a tarpaulin and a good amount of play-sand to create a large sandy area about an inch (3 cm) deep. Alternatively, a trip out to the beach or to a large public sandpit. You will also need a CD player or laptop for the music.

Suitable music can be obtained from the internet. I recommend accessing the wonderful Jamendo website[44] and searching its archive of music released under the Creative Commons licence. For this liturgy, I recommend this track by Richard Z: 'Rencontre de deux coeurs tristes'.

Or enter this link: http://bit.ly/Yi6qfn

---

44 http://www.jamendo.com/

Story

After all that had happened, those terrible past few days and now in the midst of mystery and intrigue, of wild rumour and outrageous speculation, I had just had enough. I didn't know what to think. So, Cleopas and I set off back home, to Emmaus, which isn't more than a couple of hours outside Jerusalem on foot.

As Cleopas and I walked on the dusty road, we just couldn't keep off the subject: what had happened, how our hopes that he would be the one come to save us, were dashed; and these new, scary stories …

As we were walking, another guy came up alongside us, travelling in the same direction. He seemed familiar, but I couldn't quite place him. He seemed a nice guy to walk with so we quickly fell in step and he joined our conversation.

'What are you talking about then?'

I was astounded. 'Haven't you heard about all that's been going on in the city? Have you been asleep? Have you not heard about Yeshua, the one we all hoped was the Messiah, but all our hopes were dashed as he was crucified this Passover by the Romans, and yet this morning when some of our group went to his tomb they found it empty …'

He laughed. Shaking his head, he seemed amazed by us. 'Haven't you read the Scriptures? Didn't you realize that the Messiah would need to suffer, to die and return to life?'

Well, no, actually. That wasn't what I expected at all. So he told us. He started from the very beginning and went right through the Scriptures: Moses, prophets (especially Isaiah – those two or three writers who had so much to say about the Messiah, some in poetry, some in text) and the psalms. It was amazing! Normally Bible study makes me want to go to sleep, but this guy – whoever he was – made it seem *alive*.

Well, the walk to Emmaus just seemed to fly by and the day drew on. When we got to my house, it was almost the end of the day, and the guy was about to carry on, but I wasn't going to let him travel on in the dangerous darkness.

'Come and stay with us, eat with us,' I implored him, and finally we persuaded him to join us.

We sat down for dinner, and I asked him, as our guest, to lead the prayers. As he did so, as he lifted the bread and gave God thanks for it, it was, like, suddenly clear to me, and I clicked who he was …

It was him! Only four days before, I had been in that room upstairs with him as we shared that final meal. I know that some of the other people who tell this story will only mention his closest followers, his twelve, but there were loads of us, after all, who cooked it, served it, swept up after it, and heard all he said that fateful night when he talked mysteriously about body and blood – I told Luke, I saw it with my own eyes!

It was him. The one at that last supper, the one from the cross, the one I saw put in the tomb. Dead. Here! Alive! And it hit me … Alive!

And at the moment that this realization struck me, he was gone. Disappeared. Just Cleopas and me and the families. Alive!

Well, suddenly all these rumours had foundation, all of these speculations had substance, and we had to get back to Jerusalem to tell the others what we had experienced. No matter that the day was nearly over. No matter that we put our lives at risk on the dark unlit highway back to Jerusalem – we had to get back to the upstairs room.

The journey back just rushed by and we were back in the city in no time. We burst back into the room where the twelve were and, breathlessly, Cleopas and I told our story. The twelve were amazed – as we burst in they were just talking about how he had appeared to Peter and Mary.

It was *him*. We recognized him in the breaking of the bread.

Liturgy: Walk the sand

Participants can either walk alone or in small groups up and down over the sand.

It can sometimes be a lonely road we travel down: the road is long and sometimes hazardous, carried along to a destination not of our choosing, not caring where we are led, and then we are left alone: stranded, isolated.

There is a very well-known story of a man who walks along a beach, and he glances over his shoulder and sees that in addition to his own footprints in the sand, there is another set of footprints walking beside him. He realizes that this walk on the beach is a symbol of his life and that the footprints beside him are those of God, walking with him, each step of the way.

As he looks closer, he sees that at some times in his life, there is only one set of footprints; and he recognizes those phases in his life as the times which were difficult and challenging. He turns to God and says, 'Why did you desert me in those difficult times in my life? Why did you leave me alone?'

'Ah …' says God. 'Those difficult times in your life, and the single set of footprints … those are the times when I carried you.'

Take off your shoes. Take off your socks.

Walk the sand: be conscious of the presence of God beside you. Let no one else distract you, for you begin your journey across this sand. Walk back and forth if you need.

Walk the sand: they say that a journey of a thousand miles begins with a single step.

Walk the sand: walk the lonely road.

Walk the sand: consider the times when you felt isolated and alone, condemned.

Walk the sand: feel it on your feet. Walking the sand is harder than walking on grass, more effort than walking the streets. Make the effort and walk on. Walk the sand.

There was only one set of prints in the sand. The man did not walk alone, but was carried. You do not walk alone. You walk with God.

There is no condemnation. God takes care of that. Walk on. Walk the sand.

Application

Christ walks beside us all the way through the journey of life. The 'footprints' story above has for many adults become a little overused and therefore stale, and yet young people can still be captivated by it.

The corollary of that story is where God says to the man, 'The single footprints are where I carried you, and that groove in the sand is where I had to drag you for a while.'

Paul at the Areopagus: Putting it on the line

Acts 17.16–34.

Introduction

Sometimes you just have to put your faith out there. For many of us, we won't be called to undertake TV-style debates with Richard Dawkins for example, and we might not even have to hold our own in the pub as some sneer about our faith. The best evangelism doesn't require clever words (although St Paul had plenty of those) or profound theological arguments, because the best evangelist is *you*. 'Preach the gospel,' instructed St Francis of Assisi, 'using words only if you have to', for the best sharing of the gospel is the sharing of your life, your love, your very being and the place that God has in your life. It is more attractive than all the fine words in the world.

Faith is primarily a relationship, and although thinking is vital to a healthy grown-up faith, it comes after the relationship built on an awareness of God. Treat it like an academic subject and it becomes dry, lifeless and disconnected from the experience of real people. Don't think that you have to pretend that you know everything to share faith: tell it like it is, warts and doubts and all. Of course, some (like some of the people of Athens) might scoff, but some will hear of your relationship and think, 'I'd like a bit of that: I want to hear more.'

Preparation

No equipment is required.

Story

If you had a good idea then the Areopagus ('Arry-op-ay-gus') was the place to put it to the test: the place for debate, for philosophy, which we Greeks just loved above all other pastimes. If you wanted to argue in favour of one view of life over another, then you had better be a decent senator: a skilled arguer, a better philosopher, because this was the intellectual equivalent of Fight Club, where religions faced off against each other in a battle of wit.

I'd seen some really clever people get humiliated at the Areopagus, especially when their so-called arguments just didn't stand up. Laughter and ridicule can quickly destroy a poor idea.

When they invited that guy from Tarsis who'd been causing such a stir, I thought, 'Here's another lamb to the slaughter ...'

When he stood to speak, I could see the old hands getting ready for the challenge, and unlike so many others he wasn't at all nervous. He had a certain confidence about him.

He started in a way that I wasn't expecting: most outsiders just try to have a go from the start, telling us how rubbish life, the world and everything is and how they had the solution. This bloke was different …

'I can see that the people of Athens are very religious people …'

What was this? He was complimenting us?

'… so faithful in fact that on my way here I even spotted a shrine dedicated "to an unknown God".'

That was true, I'd seen it myself, always wise to take no chances I always say, don't risk missing out any deity and getting bad luck as a result.

'… but the God who created all this isn't at all unknown, you can see the evidence of his existence in the whole of creation, and you can see how much he wants to be involved in that creation of his by sending his son into creation and proving his power by raising him from the dead.'

Well, that was some argument, and most of us were impressed with it, although there were a couple of people around me who lost it at the very last point, about God raising someone from the dead, but it seemed possible to me: the God of creation surely can overcome death? I wanted to hear more about this, and I know I was not the only one.

'I want to hear more,' I said, 'come and talk to me round at my house.'

The guy, whose name I learnt was Paul, smiled at me. 'Certainly,' he said, 'I've such an important message to share with you, and we haven't got a lot of time.'

Prayer

God, grant me the serenity to accept the things I cannot change,
The courage to change the things I can,
And wisdom to know the difference.

Reinhold Niebuhr

Application

Not everyone will be required to stand in a public space and proclaim the gospel. In fact, in this day and age, to stand on *any* street corner with a megaphone is probably not going to help.[45] The gospel is the most important message of this and any generation, and yet for it to be most effectively com-

---

45 See Rob Bell's excellent *Nooma* video 'Bullhorn', http://bit.ly/15vZgp3

municated, it is merely a whisper, just a rumour. 'Go out and proclaim the gospel,' said St Francis of Assisi, 'using words only if you have to.' The best and most persuasive argument comes through the way you respond to the needs of others, through your care for the outsider and the outcast. This is the gospel at its most persuasive – shared, not bellowed.

The Calling of the Disciples:
Oh yes we do!

Mark 3.13–19.

Introduction

A man is lost on the Devon moors. There are no signs anywhere. As he blindly goes around the twists and turns of Dartmoor, he spots a man and his sheep-dog on the side of the road. Pulling alongside him in his fancy car, he winds down the window and asks:

'Good man, how do I get to Exeter?'

The shepherd pauses for a moment.

'Well, if I was goin' to Exeter … I wudden be startin' from 'ere!'

If you were going to choose a proper set of disciples, you wouldn't start with this lot. In order to win power and influence and control you would choose the privileged, the educated, the rich. But Christ chose fishermen, outcasts, the youthful in order to reach people like you and me.

Preparation

Print out the words 'We don't need you' and 'Oh yes we do' and stick onto two large pieces of card. Even if you can only print on A4, you can 'tile' them into larger sizes by sticking them together.

For the activity you will need a quantity of modelling dough, which you can easily make using the following recipe:

- 3 cups of plain flour
- 2 tablespoons of cornflour
- 1 cup of salt
- 1 cup of cold water
- 2 teaspoons of vegetable oil
- 2 teaspoons of food colouring

Once made, this modelling dough can be stored in an airtight container for up to a week.

Story[46]

We are all different. So unique, so special. Different educations and interests, tastes in music or clothes; different ways of thinking, different ways of doing things.

And because everyone in the world was so different, so the way to reach out to the world had to be different:

- Some in the world were young and some were … more mature.
- Some in the world were clever and some were … in need of a simpler explanation. Some in the world were easily confused and some were very strong-minded.
- Some in the world were cynical and some were open.

But the Boss knew he needed them all in his world-changing team.

And each time the Boss chose someone to follow him, the others said:
We don't need you.

But the Boss said:
Oh yes, we do!

*(Get half the audience to yell out **'We don't need you'** and the other half **'Oh yes, we do'**.)*

---

46 I wrote this on my own, and then discovered it was very similar to the Barnabas Children's Bible version. Some of their phrases were better and so subconsciously as I retold and retold this, they started to merge. I can't now tell whose is whose. I give them my grateful thanks.

The Boss chose hot-headed, loud-mouthed, never-stop-to-think-about-it Peter.
And the others said: **We don't need you.**
But the Boss said: **Oh yes, we do!**

The Boss chose angel-faced, quick-to-smile, far-too-young-looking John.
And the others said: **We don't need you.**
But the Boss said: **Oh yes, we do!**

The Boss chose quick-eyed, clever-in-class, good-at-languages Andrew.
And the others said: **We don't need you.**
But the Boss said: **Oh yes, we do!**

The Boss chose grumpy-faced, stick-in-the-mud, 'I don't believe it!' Nathaniel.
And the others said: **We don't need you.**
But the Boss said: **Oh yes, we do!**

The Boss chose very-excitable, won't-ever-give-up, always-in-a-rush Philip.
And the others said: **We don't need you.**
But the Boss said: **Oh yes, we do!**

The Boss chose thoroughly-nice, his-mummy-loves-him, he'll-go-far James.
And the others said: **We don't need you.**
But the Boss said: **Oh yes, we do!**

The Boss chose good-at-maths, rather-selfish, 'I'll do anything to succeed' Matthew.
And the others said: **We don't need you.**
But the Boss said: **Oh yes, we do!**

The Boss chose never-trusting, always-doubting, 'I'm-not-sure-about-this' Thomas.
And the others said: **We don't need you.**
But the Boss said: **Oh yes, we do!**

The Boss chose not-very-strong, easily overlooked, 'I'm-too-small' James.
And the others said: **We don't need you.**
But the Boss said: **Oh yes, we do!**

The Boss chose temper-losing, tantrum-throwing, 'I'll smash your face in' Simon.
And the others said: **We don't need you.**
But the Boss said: **Oh yes, we do!**

The Boss chose very impatient, money-loving, 'I'll-do-it-my-way' Judas.
And the others said: **We don't need you.**
But the Boss said: **Oh yes, we do!**

And finally, the Boss chose nobody-special, easily overlooked, 'What's his name?' Jude.
And the others said: **We don't need you.**
But the Boss said: **Oh yes, we do!**

The Boss chose each one of these 12 disciples, with all their differences. They became a great team, working together to help the Good News reach the ends of the earth, even though Judas did let the side down a bit, and needed to be substituted by Mattias, who did a good job instead. There were lots of others as well, including some women, but we didn't always write their names down. They told lots of others, and they told others, and someone told me, and now I'm telling you, so we can continue to pass on the Good News that our lives can be sorted by him.

It doesn't matter what you've done in the past, nor what age, gender, lifestyle, income or education you have. The good news is that God has a place for you, and if all of these weirdos, these normal people, these average people, these outstanding, amazing people can come close to God through Christ, so may you.

Activity: You are special

Using the modelling dough, form different shapes, from people to rough bowls or pots. In Genesis 2, the older creation narrative sees God form mankind from the dust of the earth. In the book of Jeremiah,[47] God is the potter who shapes and moulds us.

As we create these shapes and forms, each one is unique, each one is special like us. As you create tactile shapes and forms, imagine God's hands shaping you: not just at the beginning of your life, but through all your life, continually perfecting you.

Even if there are things about you which make you unhappy, know that God and God working through you continually forms and reforms you. In his eyes you are perfect already, because he made you like that, but that perfection continues.

---

47 Jeremiah 18.1–18.

Brother Andrew

Introduction

Young people often feel disempowered by the society and culture around them. They fear that they are unable to make significant change to anything: that the problems of the world, or even in their own lives, are beyond their capability. Yet, God calls each of them to the extraordinary. When Mother Teresa of Calcutta was asked how she might possibly feed all the poor of the slums, she replied. 'One at a time.' The story of Brother Andrew shows how personal, individual action can have a profound effect; sometimes 'One at a time' is the best way for real change to be made. It begins with ourselves and ends in the Kingdom of God.

Preparation

Equipment: A collection of Bibles, from beautiful family Bibles to worn and tattered pamphlet Bibles, easily picked up from junk shops, study Bibles and youth Bibles that you have in stock for working with young people. If you have a Greek New Testament or an Interlinear Bible, then even better. Pile them up in teetering, haphazard stacks.

Story

It wasn't so long ago that huge parts of Europe were cut off, excluded from what was going on in the world, all because of politics, power and fear. After the Second World War Europe was effectively cut in half, between Communist Russia and Western Europe. A wall was even built that divided the German capital of Berlin so people couldn't run away to the West and a bit more freedom.

It was hard and brutal living behind what Winston Churchill described as 'an Iron Curtain' – there wasn't a literal iron curtain (other than that wall in Berlin) but that's how it felt. One of the things that Communist countries feared the most was faith: it detracted from their political ideals, and even hugely devout countries such as Russia, Poland and Romania found that churches were persecuted and shut down, their priests and pastors forced to celebrate the liturgy and lead worship in secret. The Bible itself effectively became a banned book.

And why not? For this collection of writings contains the very essence of freedom, the struggle of people against oppression, hope for the downtrodden and rescue for the lost. Throughout all the many and varied writings in these Holy Scriptures, oppressed peoples the world over have seen the promise that God offers to them and the solution that is Jesus. Of course the Communists feared it. Of course it was banned.

One young man from Holland thought that the banning of the Bible in these Communist countries was very wrong. His name was Andrew: a faithful man with a deep love of God's holy word.

He visited some of these Communist countries and was shocked to discover how difficult it was to get hold of a Bible and yet people were desperate to read of God. Bibles were hidden, shared secretively, treasured. Without a thought he gave his own Bible away to someone, and it dawned on him how important it was to get God's word out to the people. He filled a suitcase with Bibles and came back. He did it again. And again. He became 'God's Smuggler'.

A couple of times he got into trouble. Occasionally his camper-van stuffed with Bibles that churches had bought for him to just give away was found by the Communists and taken from him. Once his passport got stamped with 'Do not let this man back into our country', and 'Brother' Andrew as they called him thought the project was over. A man who worked at the border (for the same country that had just banned Brother Andrew) gently suggested that he should cross between Belgium and Holland (both non-Communist countries) and make sure that his banned passport was stamped each time so that it would fill up and he could get a new one without the 'banned' stamp in. Clearly some were delighted that Brother Andrew wanted to share God's word with the people!

For many years Andrew worked in secret, supported by churches in the West. He set up a secret network that shared Bibles, giving them away to anyone who wanted to know more. Eventually, Communism fell apart, perhaps because people of faith started to stand up and be counted, and most of these countries have emerged into freedom, where faith can be practised openly. Andrew was a part of that. Clearly, one man giving away Bibles couldn't defeat massive countries like Russia, but God always favours the small man, like David against Goliath. It is all too easy to shy away from doing something to make the world a better place because, 'Well, I'm just one person', but with faith you can make a difference, and change happens because people get involved.

You might not have to do something that dramatic, and yet what does God call you to stand up for? What little action for what is right might make a small but significant difference in this world?

Activity: Bible

Explore the variety of Bibles. You might want to note how every Bible we have is a translation from the Greek (and Hebrew) that the Bible was originally written in, which means that making sense of what God is saying to us in the Bible will always be a process of translation and will require us to seek understanding of Scripture through the Holy Spirit.

This does not diminish the importance of Scripture in a healthy and vital spiritual life, but rather requires that we work harder with it: ask serious questions of it and of God and understand the context of what is written. Many of our earliest Greek manuscripts where written ALLINCAPITAL-LETTERSWITHOUTSPACESORPUNCTUATION and so we must be very careful, for example, to avoid putting in meanings from punctuation that doesn't exist. A good example would be Luke 23.43. Consider the difference in a simple comma: 'Truly I say to you, today you will be with me in Paradise' and 'Truly I say to you today, you will be with me in Paradise'. That comma is not in the original text. I think using a variety of translations of Scripture is useful, because through them you can see (and hear) many different nuances.

Prayer for Guidance

Speak, Lord, your servants are listening.
Through your Holy Scripture, through your Holy Church, through your
   Holy Spirit,
you come to us and fill us with the fire of your love.
May our hearts burn with desire as we hear your truth revealed to us.
May our lives shine out as we reflect your love.
May we be open to hear your word,
leading us through all of life's journey.
Through Jesus Christ, our Lord. Amen.

5

Change and Transformation

Working in the Vineyard: You have worth

Matthew 20.1–16.

Introduction

In harsh economic times, the story of the workers in the vineyard seems even more relevant than before.

Preparation

No preparation is required. You can create a quiet sacred space for the meditation by dimming the lights and lighting an old Pascal Candle or two.[48] These large candles can create a really lovely, warm atmosphere.

---

48 A good use for the Easter Candle which usually gets discarded. They are very large and most churches don't know what to do with them, so they store them away largely unburnt. Why not make use of them for this mission?

Story

It's not easy being unemployed. I don't know if you, your parents, or someone you know – maybe older brothers or sisters have known what it is like to be out of work. It's difficult. It's soul-destroying. Looking for work, no matter how hard you try, can be hard: hearing the words 'No' or 'Sorry' over and over again can cut to your very soul, and undermine your sense of self-worth.

So there we were, hanging around the Job Centre, hanging out really because there was no work to be found. Up comes the Boss of a massive vineyard: a beautiful place which we all know of hereabouts and he calls over to a bunch of likely workers:

'Hey, I need you.'

The Boss chooses first the ones who are clearly the best: the fittest, the toughest, the ones who'll do a solid day's work for a solid day's pay.

'One coin?' The going rate for a day's work these days. 'Of course,' they say, eager for the chance to work, the chance to eat for today.

The rest of us are left behind. No surprises there, really. For the past few years I've had this bad leg and it makes me walk a bit funny, and so I'm always the one who misses out. In school I was the last one to be picked for games, and in my adult life, well let's just say these games are the difference between starving and subsisting.

A little later, he comes back again. He needs more workers. He chooses them and away they go with him. Lucky beggars.

Once more, he's back. 'I still need more people – you, you and you.' Not me again. All that are left now are the unfit, the unhealthy, the dirty and the dim.

Towards the end of the day, only a few more hours of daylight left, he is back again and now he is pointing at me. 'Come on, I have more work to do in this place, and I need YOU.'

'Me?' Surely not? 'Me? I haven't worked for …'

'Yes, you. And you, and you,' and in turn he gathers the rest of us who are otherwise no good for anything and takes us to the vineyard. He wanted *me*.

For the first time in many years I felt valued, wanted. He set me to work, and hard work it was. But I put my back into it simply because I was exhilarated to be wanted. It was only an hour or so of work, but it felt good to be making a difference.

At the end of the day, we formed a queue to be paid. Those of us who'd come at the end were the first in line, and when I got to the Boss, he hands me one coin: the coin that he promised to those blokes at the beginning of the day. I was so proud to earn my keep, pay my way, do something. I would have framed that coin if I didn't need the money so much. It felt like much more than just the security that a bit of cash offered.

We all got the same. All those who started with me got the coin. Then the next batch. The guys who'd worked all day were clearly expecting a bonus if we at the end of the day had got a coin: after all, they'd worked at least twice as hard … and yet when they got to the table, the Boss proffered the same coin to them.

'Hang on …' they said, 'we've done more than them.'

'Didn't we agree one coin?' the Boss asked. 'What is it to you what I pay the others?'

I realized then that the coin he had given me showed that he valued me, that he valued my work. But it wasn't about what I did for it, it was more of a mark of his generosity, a symbol of his outrageous care for people even like me. It made me feel worth something.

It doesn't matter really where you are in this world. It doesn't matter how good or how bad you've been in the past, or how worthy or unworthy you think yourself of God's love. He calls you. He calls you to come and work for him. To come and do his will and build his Kingdom, to change this world into a better place … and he does it because he values you.

The coin he offers is not a shiny piece of hard currency, but a far greater currency: eternal life, offered to all, without barriers.

Come and work for the Boss.

Meditation: God calls

You are special. You are valued.
For what you are.
For what you can be.
No matter what you have done,
No matter from where you have come.

You are called by God –
Yes, you.
As you are.
To what you will be.

You are special and God loves that in you.
Be whom God calls you to be.
Be you.
Be called.

The Last Supper: The first meal

Matthew 26.20–35; Mark 14.12–31; Luke 22.7–38; John 13.1–17, 26.

Introduction

In my first two books my key point was that mission and sacraments are essentially linked. The sacramental life isn't a reward for coming to a 'correct' decision at the end of a road of discipleship but aids the process of discipleship. The Eucharistic encounter is not an optional extra in the life of faith, but an essential expression of it.

Preparation

You should have a table laid out as though for the Eucharist: chalice, paten, pitta bread or a tortilla wrap and a bottle of wine, apple or blackcurrant juice. If we take seriously the teaching of Christ, then the story of the Last Supper will be one of the most important you tell. I deliberately use the same kind of phrasing that I use when celebrating the Eucharist to make the connection clear. I handle a paten and a chalice as I am telling the story, tear a piece of bread and pour out some real wine (or it could be apple juice or blackcurrant – this isn't a Eucharist but a retelling).

Story

Whenever something important needs to be celebrated, then food is shared.

Think of all the great birthday parties you have celebrated: surrounded by friends and family, laughter and cheers, jelly and ice cream. Think of those sumptuous Christmas dinners: the table groaning with all that meat and all the trimmings, crackers and Christmas pudding and your family all around.

When people come together for something special, then food is often involved. To share food says, 'I think you are special', and no matter where in the world, no matter what the culture, and even no matter what the religion, the sharing of food is always a mark of hospitality and friendship.

We had eaten so many meals together in the past three years: from banquets offered by the great and the good to going hungry together in desolate places, from feeding to our fill on the mountain (or was it the plain? My memory gets a little hazy sometimes, we did so much with him) to sharing what little we had with the poor and the destitute, our common table seemed to signify our common life. We ate, we laughed, we talked: sometimes about the most profound thought-provoking stuff and sometimes trivial rubbish or silly arguments about which one of us was stronger, or cleverer or more holy or even a better mate of his …

So this meal, this Passover meal was just like all the others. Don't think for a moment that it was a miserable meal, a solemn occasion, a boring event. We joked, we laughed, we talked the usual inane rubbish, and then in the middle of it, just as he was about to launch into the bread course, as he did the usual prayers he said something that has stayed with me for ever …

'Take, eat, this is my body which is given for you. Do this and I will be present with you always.'[49]

It was a bit shocking really … eat his flesh? Cannibalism? We had strict laws about that kind of thing – even if it was only a metaphor, it was an offensive one because the eating of another human was and still is so taboo, so wrong, so illegal and yet he was adamant about it: eat not just *with* me … but eat me.

You could see that his words had disturbed many of us around the table; in the flickering light of the oil lamps I could see Pete had gone quite white. Then he continued.

He took the cup of wine: a big single cup that we shared as a sign of our togetherness, and again he said the prayer of thanks that we had grown up with. Looking round the table he continued:

Take this all of you and drink from it. This is my blood. The blood which seals a new agreement between God and the world. It is shed for you and for all so that your sins may be forgiven. Do this and I will be present with you always.

Chilling. It sounded as if he was going away from us, and yet was keen for us to see that he was with us in spirit. Where was he going? He'd said nothing about going away before!

As he handed out the bread to us, it seemed now to be more than just food. It had significance and meaning. As the cup passed between us, and I drank deeply from it,

---

49 'Remembrance' is such a weak word in English and does not capture what Jesus is trying to say here. The word he uses ἀνάμνησις (Strong's 364, see http://biblesuite.com/greek/364.htm) means 'bring me into the presence of'. Your Eucharistic theology might just want to consign this to a fond recalling of a past event, but for others the Real Presence of Christ in the Eucharist is an echo of ancient libations and sacrifices: deeper connections from the past, present and future.

although it tasted the same, it *felt* different. It felt as though it was doing something different within me, and I was somehow changed by it. I never felt closer to him as I did at that moment.

I didn't understand what he meant by it. Bread and wine ... body and blood. It made little sense to me on the night and even now, if I am to be honest, I don't understand it. He said to continue breaking this bread, and I have. Wherever I have got to, whenever I have met new followers I have said the same things as he said to us that night. When I do that, it feels like ... just as he said ... that he is there around the table. When we eat and drink, that simple everyday act proclaims him, recalls those terrible events that were so quickly to follow that night, and I will keep doing it until he comes again in glory.

I don't think I will ever understand it. It's a mystery beyond anything I have ever encountered, and I'm happy just to experience it, and the difference it makes to me rather than getting my head around it.

Two thousand years hence and we still have only the barest inkling of what it really means. All the prayers of the saints, all the words of all the theologians across the centuries, and we still haven't got our heads around this mystery.

When you eat normal food, it becomes a part of you, it becomes absorbed into you, and then is got rid of in the usual way; yet when you eat of this bread and drink of this wine, you become a part of him, a communion, a joining. You can't pull these wafers apart and see real flesh, and yet Christ is here. You can't push a microscope into it, and point to something and say 'There! There is God!' and yet, Christ is present. You can't see the wind blowing, but you can see the effect of the wind blowing on the trees; in the same way, look not for body or blood but see the effect that his blessed sacraments have on those who receive it.

Look for the effect that it has on *you*.

Activity: The Sacrament

If you have an amenable priest to hand, the celebration of the Eucharist seems most appropriate. For many ideas for creative Eucharistic liturgies with children, please see my earlier book: *Creative Ideas for Sacramental Worship with Children.*[50]

---

50 S. Rundell, *Creative Ideas for Sacramental Worship with Children*, Canterbury Press: Norwich, 2011.

Application

Matt Maher wrote a wonderfully atmospheric and profound worship song on the Eucharist called 'Remembrance'. This video combining that song with images from *Jesus Christ Superstar* can be useful to set the scene:

or enter the link: http://bit.ly/UjEzXa

Transfiguration: Everything changes

Luke 9.28–36; Mark 9.1–8; Matthew 17.1–6.

Introduction

Once again, my biblical hero Peter says things without thinking and reveals untold truths in the exposure of his crassness. This means there is hope for us all. There is a lot of Peter in me, and I bet just a little of his impetuosity, his directness and his profound trust in something he couldn't *quite* grasp in you as well.

Preparation

No preparation is required.

Story

'C'mon Pete' he said, 'let's go up the mountain!'

Following Jesus meant that no two days were the same as we moved from mountains to plains, from lakeshore to village to city. He was constantly on the move, preaching and healing without let-up. It was so tiring – for all of us: I could see he needed a break, a pause, an opportunity to pray and reboot.

There were just the four of us: himself, Jimmy and Jonny and myself. The others stayed down in the village below the mountain, kicking back and getting their own rest. We get up the top of Tabor and then *everything* changes.

I'd seen a lot in the past two years of our journey, of our adventure: healings and miracles, coincidences and stuff that was just plain weird; but this takes the biscuit. The place is filled with light and Jimmy and Jonny and I turn around and see he is somehow *changed* – he has become the source of light itself, coming from out of him and almost blinding us. It was … transfiguring.

I can make out in the bright light two other people besides him, and so I have to shield my eyes like you do when you look towards the sun. To my squinting eyes, I can make them out and in my heart I know who they are.

Jimmy behind me exclaims 'Moses … Elijah!' and we all realize that at the same time we have come to know who they are. He has given us a glimpse of who he *really* is, and to whom he is connected – the fathers of our faith.

They appear to be talking, and as we are there in his presence it strikes me that this must be what heaven is a bit like: a glimpse of what it is to be in God's awesome presence. There is no distraction, no panic, just calm … just warmth. I was happier than I had ever been in my life. And I didn't want it to end.

It just came out of my mouth.

'Boss – let me set up the tents for you and Moses and Elijah!'

I know it sounds a bit dumb, but you see, by the rules of hospitality, if Moses and Elijah accept our invitation they have to stay until *we* say the party ends, and I never wanted it to end!

As soon as I said it, I knew that I had ruined it. The light faded from him and the figures (Jimmy and I are convinced it was Moses and Elijah, Jonny isn't so sure it was *them* but he'll go along with us) faded from sight and then … it was just us.

I felt in my heart like I'd heard the voice of God – that he was pleased with the Boss. It was just the most awesome moment. It could have been a minute or an hour or a whole day, I didn't care: it was an encounter with the living God and I would never be the same again.

He swore us to secrecy, not to share it with anyone. Then we went down the mountain to the towns and the plains to get on with the work he had called us to do. It was only a moment, but it would be with me my whole life.

Everything changed. He changed. I was changed.

Prayer

Let us go up to the mountain top.
Let us go up to the place where the land meets the sky,
where the earth touches heaven,
to the place of encounter,
to the place of swirling mist,
to the place of voices and conversations,
to the place of listening.

O God,
we open our eyes and we see Jesus,
the months of ministry transfigured to a beam of light,
the light of the world,
your light.
May your light shine upon us.

We open our eyes and we see Moses and Elijah,
your word restoring us,
showing us the way,
telling a story,
your story, his story, our story.
May your word speak to us.

We open our eyes and we see mist,
the cloud of your presence
which assures us of all we do not know
and that we do not need to fear.
Teach us to trust.

We open our eyes and we see Peter,
his best plans, our best plans,
our missing the point,
our missing the way.
Forgive our foolishness and sin.

We open our eyes and we see Jesus,
not casting us off,
but leading us down, leading us out –
to ministry, to people.
Your love endures for ever.

We open our ears and we hear your voice,
'This is my beloved Son, listen to him!'
And we give you thanks.

Amen.

Lazarus: The second chance

John 11.1–46.

Introduction

The story of the raising of Lazarus is a prelude to the resurrection of Christ himself and the most powerful illustration of the power of God over sin and death. It was the point in Christ's life when his enemies finally determined to kill him. To heal some people, to tell some good stories, this was benign, but to start challenging death – this really upset the authorities! This is why the good news of Jesus is both transformative and radical and why it really gets up the noses of those who claim earthly power.

Preparation

No preparation is required.

Story

Without my brother Lazarus, my sister and I would be out on the street, or worse. When he became sick, we were worried both for him and for ourselves. We'd given our lives to caring for first our aged parents and now our brother, and until now we'd had no worries. Society doesn't look kindly on people like us – unmarried – and we would be quickly reduced to poverty, homelessness and then starvation as there was no work we could do, no income and no future.

It all suddenly seemed so terrifying.

We sent for him, knowing that he would come and would sort his beloved friend out. He had been a good friend to us and Mary had spent all that time at his feet, listening to his teaching, drinking in his words. At the time it had annoyed me as it left me to do all the work, but even though I was busy, I was listening to all that he said: 'The better part,' he'd described it as.

But where was he? We'd said how urgent it was, and yet he was ... delayed. The days dragged on as Lazarus, my dear brother, continued to slip away, to be brought to another shore, and an eternal comfort.

When he died, it was as though my heart had been ripped out. I felt so empty. We did the usual burial rites and placed him in the tomb amid our tears and our cries of loss. We sealed the tomb with a large stone as securely as our fate was sealed: nothing stretched out before us.

On the fourth day after we had lost Lazarus, he arrived. He went straight to the place of burial.

And wept.

Such tears. Such sorrow.

Yet my sorrow had turned to anger at his delay. I knew that if he had been here it would have all been different. I lashed out against him with harsh words and tears and recriminations and the beating of weakened fists on his great muscular chest.

'If you had been here ... if only you had been here ...'

He was calm. My outpouring of pent-up grief seemed to displace his own. 'He will rise again,' he says.

'Rise again, oh yes, I know all that "on the day of resurrection" – all pie-in-the-sky, jam-tomorrow sort of rubbish that the priests all tell you. No problem,' I sniff.

'Not jam-tomorrow, but now …' he replies, 'remove the stone!'

We looked at each other in disbelief. He died four days ago. This is a hot country … the smell … it would be unimaginable!

He was insistent, so we did what he asked. Did he want to pray right by the body? Somehow make up for his tardiness?

When the stone was removed, he looked heavenward and prayed, crying out 'Lazarus! Come out!'

What happened then was like a blur. There were shouts, cries, tears, terror and then disbelief and joy as, staggering out of the tomb, wrapped in the shroud was … Lazarus!

We rushed over and unwrapped him, tears of grief transformed into tears of joy. Lazarus was in tears also: of relief, of gratitude, of faith. Our lives were changed from that moment on and each day would be treasured as precious. So often we treat our lives as though they are nothing, without value or worth. You really don't appreciate what you have until it is gone, and then to have it restored back to you is to help you to make the most of it.

Each new dawn is filled with promise. Each sunset heavy with gratitude. As the three of us in this family grow old together we will treasure each day, each moment and make sure that nothing is wasted. The second chance he gave to us needs to be shared with the world.

Prayer: For a fresh start each day

Each new day
may I pause as I begin this new day
to give it to you, Lord.
Before the rush of life breaks in;
before life crashes in through my still sleepy mind;
let me hold your promise of new life.
Keep me from slipping back
for I know that what is forgiven is as if it never were.
Each new day, your grace gives me a fresh start to walk in your light again.

May the Lord support us all the day long,
till the shadows lengthen and the evening comes,
the busy world is hushed,
the fever of life is over,

and our work is done.
Then in his mercy may he give us a safe place to come home to,
a holy rest,
and peace at the last.

Amen.

Zaccheus: Change happens through encounter

Luke 19.1–10.

Introduction

The overarching narrative of the Christian faith is that life can and is trans-formed by God: that past mistakes can be learned from and that nobody is beyond the love and forgiveness of Christ. As young people strive to make their own way in this world, to become aware of themselves and their possi-bilities and to explore what it means to be human, mistakes will be made. This is not something which parents, youth leaders or priests can prevent, for growing and learning involves the making of bad choices and moving on from them: experience matters. We might be able to take the edges off some of the worst choices, and need to always be there to support them through the worst of those still made, but it is unconditional love which will be the great-est support on life's journey: modelled on the unconditional love the Father shows to us all.

Change is possible. Change happens when one encounters Christ.

Preparation

No preparation is required.

Story

I'm not the most popular man around these parts. I title myself 'Zachheus the tax collector, Jericho division' but what I hear behind my back is much worse, 'Zach the thief', 'Zach the cheat', 'Zach the guy who feathers his own nest by cheating the rest of us'. I suppose there is a bit of truth in all that, but you have to make a bit of cash where you can, and a bit of a hustle is – well, what everyone does don't they, so why shouldn't I? But every time I stole a bit more, twisted a few more figures and used some of my boys to extort a bit more from the poor, I felt a little bit more isolated, a little bit more lost. It was more than people just avoiding me and my company, it was like I was venturing out on my own ... and by now I felt I didn't know the way back. It was like getting lost ...

Now, I'm not the tallest of people, and in a crowd all I get to see is the back of people's knees, so when I heard that he was coming through Jericho, when I heard the stories about him, the amazing way he taught and the wonderful things he did – curing the sick and the mad, the lame, the poor and reaching out to everyone, well I wasn't going to miss out on this – the most entertaining thing to happen in Jericho since, well ... Joshua and the battle!

In keeping with this growing reputation of his, the streets were rammed with people. There was no way I could see over them and well, no one was going to let me through because frankly, everyone hated me and what I stood for – the occupation of our land by those brutal money-grabbing Romans. That's when I saw the tree, and, ever one to take the chance, I climbed up it.

It was a good view, and I could see the commotion down the street as he was coming – the buzz and excitement. People below me were talking about what he might do – a healing or some more of those amazing stories about God's plans for us. He passed right under me, and I felt a little shudder as though my conscience – something which I haven't heard from in a long time – had suddenly reawakened, and I thought for a second about my life and what I did with it.

As that happened, he stopped. Right under me. Then he looked up – straight at me – there could be no doubt that it was me he was regarding!

'Zaccheus – come on down ... let's eat at your place tonight!' he said. How did he know I was there? How did he know my name?

My place? No one has wanted to share my hospitality since I started collecting taxes for the Romans! I was wondering where all the spare crockery was – my place?

That caused a bit of a stir. All the great and good of Jericho were hoping that he would share their table, have the prestige of the great teacher in their house; and now he was asking me ... me? The outcast? Me? The sinner?

I scrambled down the tree, and the people parted around me. I suppose they thought of me as a little bit tainted by the taxes I stole off them. With a bit of a shrug I led him and his followers to my house.

It was a great evening: we ate, we talked, he talked and he taught and for once I listened. All those preachers in the synagogue talked all the time, but it never touched me, neither here in my head nor in my heart. But this did.

Towards the end, something just snapped in me.

'Listen – I've done a lot of wrong things, and I'm going to make amends. If I have cheated anyone I will pay them back and some more besides, and as for the rest of all this … I'll give half of it to the poor. From now on it'll be different!'

He smiled at me. That meant an awful lot, because as he looked at me, I could see that he knew that I had got it.

He laughed, 'Salvation is here. This is what I came for … to bring back the lost!'

And I knew that I was not lost any more.

Prayer: For the lost

Let us pray …

We pray for those who do not yet know Christ. If there is anyone we have on our hearts and in our minds, we lift them up to you, Lord.

We pray that God will draw them to himself.
'*No one can come to me unless the Father who sent me draws him*' (John 6.44).

That they themselves would seek to know God.
'*But if from there you seek the Lord your God, you will find him if you look for him with all your heart and with all your soul*' (Deuteronomy 4.29).

For the Holy Spirit to work in them.
'*When the Holy Spirit comes he will convict the world of guilt in regard to sin and righteousness … But when he, the Spirit of truth, comes, he will guide you into all truth*' (John 16.8, 13).

That they would believe in Christ as Saviour.
'I tell you the truth, whoever hears my word and believes him who sent me has eternal life' (John 5.24).

That they would take root and grow in Christ.
'So then, just as you received Christ Jesus as Lord, continue to live in him, rooted and built up in him, strengthened in the faith as you were taught, and overflowing with thankfulness' (Colossians 2.6, 7).

There is no one lost from Christ. For those we have named in our hearts. Amen.

The Good Samaritan: Making a difference

Luke 10.29–37.

Introduction

Social media enables people all over the world to communicate instantly. Ideas which used to take centuries to cross continents in the past are now disseminated globally in minutes. Concepts, jokes and those pearls of wisdom percolated into 'memes' form and reform as they spread across different cultures and time zones. The meaning of 'neighbour' which Jesus had already opened out so widely is even wider now, and yet remains firmly within the warm embrace of God.

Preparation

Soup ingredients

- 200 g chopped raw vegetables, such as onions, celery and carrots. Any vegetables seem to work, in my experience
- 300 g potatoes
- 1 tbsp oil

- 700 ml stock (one or two vegetable stock cubes dissolved in hot water)
- crème fraîche and fresh herbs as garnish.

Story

This bloke was going through a rough part of town. It wasn't his town, and he didn't really belong here. You can think of your own local tensions: football teams, chav and grunge, colour of skin, there's no end of examples. Whatever it was, he was out on his own, in a vulnerable place, in the wrong place.

He got set upon, beaten, robbed and left in a bleeding, bruised pile on the pavement.

As our victim was lying there, he thought he could see someone coming down the street dressed in a dog-collar – the local priest – he was saved! But the local priest had so much on his mind, Masses to say and masses to do and he just looked past the man on the ground – a head so far in the clouds that he couldn't see the need in front of him.

A little while later, our victim lying there with bruised and swollen eyes thought he could see one of his own – the same football shirt, the same dress code, the same hairstyle or cap or whatever we choose to show our individuality by being just like all our mates – he was saved! But his brother in fashion didn't want to get blood on him, didn't want to get involved, didn't want to put aside his plans for the day and deal with it – his life was already far too full to bother with this need.

When the victim thought that was it, that the end was near, there came another standing over him. Different. Different colour football shirt, different colour skin, different style of music coming over the iPod. Different. This means trouble, this means the end.

But the stranger, the man who had no ties to our victim, was the one to help him up, to get him to the hospital, to sort out the paperwork and the police, to help the victim get his life back together. He went out of his own way to make a difference to the victim, went the extra mile.

Which of these three, asked Jesus, *was like a neighbour?*

The one who showed him kindness, they answered. Not the one whom everyone expects to be holy. Not the one who seemed to be from the same family, the same mindset, the same tribe. The one who looked beyond the badges and the labels and saw the need of another human being.

Jesus then gave those to whom he told this story a simple command:

Go then, and do likewise.

Activity

Make soup. It takes time, but then again so does the discipleship of a soul. You can start the soup at the beginning of a night or event, and share it out at the end. It is even better if you can share the soup with people outside your group: perhaps decant it into some flasks and disposable cups and take it out onto the streets, or take it round to a local project.

The amazing thing about soup is that it can be made from all kinds of random vegetables, thrown in together and left to simmer. The result is, often surprisingly, tasty and nutritious. It therefore makes an excellent metaphor for community: a random collection of people who over time can create something beautiful. It is also best shared. It is Christ who is the Stock which holds it all together.

Soup Method

- Depending on the age and aptitude of your group, you might encourage some to help with the peeling and chopping. Supervision and appropriate hygiene should be employed.
- Fry the chopped raw vegetables with the potatoes, peeled and cubed, in a little oil for a few minutes until they begin to soften.
- Cover with the stock and simmer for 10–15 minutes until the vegetables are tender. Everyone can have a hand in stirring.
- Blend until smooth (again, fun for everyone in the group to have a go at), then season with pepper and salt and perhaps some Tabasco or Worcester-shire sauce according to taste.
- Serve with a dollop of crème fraîche and some fresh herbs.
- You can freeze it for up to one month.

Application

Goodness does not necessarily mean holiness. You can try to be so religious, so caught up in the ways of doing the Church that you miss what the point is. You can be looking so hard for God on the inside that you forget that some-times God needs you to share that gift with others.

A life of faith can make a wonderful difference deep in your own life, but if you keep it there it will make no difference in this world. The gift of faith is not something selfish, but something to be given out through you to others. All others. All kinds. All ways. All perspectives. All are part of God's wonderful creation and all are worthy of God's grace, his kindness and his goodness, through you.

You can make a difference. So as he said: *Go then, and do likewise.*

Victory and Vindication

David and Goliath: With God on your side there is nothing to be afraid of

1 Samuel 17.

Introduction

The Christian story has inspired so many people to amazing acts of bravery: to stand up for what they believed in and against injustice and oppression, to face their own deaths for what they passionately believed in. The final section of this resource turns to the message that with God in your life, there is *nothing* to be afraid of.

Preparation

No preparation is required.

Story

The two great armies faced each other: the people of the area known as Philistia and the people of Israel. As they looked at each other across the valley, the taunting and the showing off began.

   The biggest man the Israelites had *ever* seen came out from the line of the Philistines: at least twice as big as any Israelite soldier, more muscle, a better tan, a much bigger sword. The massive man's name was Goliath and he began to taunt: 'Come on! Who wants a piece of me? Come and have a go … One on one – I'll take on the best you've got, you puny, measly Israelites.'

The Israelites took one look at the huge soldier, and they were *terrified*.

I mean *really, really scared*, wobbly legs, shaky tummy, the lot.

King Saul, king of the Israelites, looked over his wobbly army and asked 'Is there anyone who is prepared to fight the big man?'

And they all looked away, embarrassed, ashamed.

Goliath now started to brag: 'Ah, you're all cowards … it just goes to show that your God's a load of rubbish.' The pride in his bragging really hurt the Israelites.

From the back of the Israelite army a small, indignant voice rang out, 'I'm not standing for that – you can't say that about God!' The voice was angry.

It wasn't even from a proper soldier: it was a young boy who had brought some sandwiches for his brothers on the front line.

King Saul asked the young boy his name. 'David, son of Jesse – and I'm prepared to fight him – I'm not scared,' he cried bravely.

Well, no one else was prepared to, so Saul called his armourers and they started to kit out the young boy in the finest Israelite leather armour. It was useless: he was so small that he looked swamped in it. All of the other soldiers couldn't help it, but they burst out laughing. David felt a bit silly in all that gear. He threw it off, 'I don't need this, I just need my slingshot and my faith in God,' he cried.

Picking up a couple of sharp stones and loading one into his sling, he stepped out in front of the big, sweaty, aggressive Goliath.

'Who's this?' asked Goliath scornfully. 'Prepare to be squashed!' Goliath yelled as he started to swing his massive sword.

David, who didn't have a heavy sword or cumbersome armour, was much more nimble than Goliath. He sidestepped the slow, heavy (yet scary) sword and let fly with his slingshot.

'Crack!' The stone caught Goliath on the forehead, and he was stunned for a second. Dazed, he dropped his sword. David let fly another stone – just like he did every day when he was scaring off the wolves and hyenas from his sheep, and once again …

'Crack!' Another bullseye shot and Goliath went down. Stone dead.

You should have heard the Israeli army. They jumped for joy – the small boy with faith had overcome the big bully with attitude. Their bravery flooded back and they jumped in to attack. The Philistines, shocked and stunned by the sight of their top soldier crumpling so easily, took fright and ran away.

Victory to Israel. Victory for those who trusted that God would give them strength to overcome what scared them most. Victory for the little person.

Application

It doesn't matter what it is that stands before us: it doesn't have to be a real enemy, a soldier, a bully. It might be just our fears that we have to overcome. It may be an anxiety, or something that we have to get around which prevents us from moving forward.

Fear of that enemy can stop us in our tracks, paralyze us and make us feel that nothing we can do can overcome the great enemy before us.

Yet God will give us the equipment we need to deal with what challenges us. It may be something quite small, but as we have heard, something small can overcome even the biggest bully, if we stand up to it.

God doesn't really like war or fighting, although so many people have gone to war believing that God was on their side, but he won't ever stand on the side of a bully. There are other ways to overcome your challenges than with violence, and the stones he will give you will be stones of courage, wit, bravery and cunning, and there is no Goliath in your life that cannot be brought down.

The Cross: It is sorted

Matthew 26.30—27.56; Mark 14.26—15.47; Luke 22.39—23.56; John 18.1—19.42.

Introduction

There are so many different ways to retell the crucifixion of the Lord that a whole book could not contain them.[51] I want to return to the finest framework for retelling that key story: the Stations of the Cross. It is story, reflection and activity in one. I have heard it told from many different perspectives, through the eyes of Isaiah or the psalmist, with modern music or from the perspective of those who saw him pass by.[52]

---

51 John 21.25.
52 M. Anderson and P. Heesome, *What a Day: Stations of the Cross for Young People*, Kevin Mayhew, 1998 – a most excellent resource in which all people, young and old, can read/perform a station from the perspective of a passer-by.

I lead the Stations of the Cross with children over a wide range of ages, from primary school to teenagers and young adults. Clearly no single retelling will suit all ages. The graphic and unavoidably cruel nature of the cross should of course be tailored to your audience and where they are in their spiritual journey. It's not a nice story. If we over-sanitize for every age group then we denude it of its power and its significance. However, you don't need to be over-explicit or graphic: all ages can to an extent identify with shame, humiliation and an inkling of our mistreatment of Christ reflected in behaviour in the playground.

Preparation

You need to obtain or access some images of the Stations of the Cross. There are so many to choose from in all styles, cultures and traditions. Some churches, of course, come with Stations of the Cross already in situ, or you might want to search out some from the internet. If you have space, you can place them on the walls and walk from point to point around the edge of a church or a large hall. If space and numbers don't permit it, you can remain static and illustrate each station with a PowerPoint graphic or hold up an image.

On the CD there is a series of Stations of the Cross painted by Clare Williams and these are used to illustrate this section.[53]

Story

Almost since the crucifixion, people have travelled on pilgrimage to Jerusalem, to walk through the old city and to imagine walking with Christ on the Via Dolorosa, or *way of sorrows*. Throughout the city, at various points or stations, the story is retold. Not everyone will be able to make the pilgrimage to Jerusalem, but we can go on a pilgrimage in this place, travel in our minds to Jerusalem and walk behind Christ.

Traditionally, at the start of each individual station, we say:

We adore you, O Christ and we praise you.
Because by your holy cross, you have redeemed the world.

---

53 Used with permission of the artist. The originals of these Stations are available to be used by churches. Please contact the artist on clarebear_e@hotmail.com.

Each station may end with a traditional prayer: the Lord's Prayer, the Agnus Dei, the Glory Be or the Hail Mary.

Lord's Prayer

Our Father, who art in heaven
Hallowed be Thy Name;
Thy kingdom come,
Thy will be done,
on earth as it is in heaven.
Give us this day our daily bread,
and forgive us our trespasses,
as we forgive those who trespass against us;
and lead us not into temptation,
but deliver us from evil. Amen.

Agnus Dei

Lamb of God, you take away the sin of the world, have mercy on us.
Lamb of God, you take away the sin of the world, have mercy on us.
Lamb of God, you take away the sin of the world, grant us peace.

Glory Be

Glory be to the Father, and to the Son and to the Holy Spirit:
as it was in the beginning, is now, and shall be for ever, world without end. Amen.

Hail Mary

Hail Mary, full of grace, the Lord is with thee.
Blessed art thou and blessed is the fruit of thy womb, Jesus.
Holy Mary, Mother of God, pray for us sinners now and at the hour of our death. Amen.

First Station: Pilate condemns Jesus

Pilate certainly had a reputation as a cruel man: a ruthless governor unafraid to use the might of Rome to ensure peace and the payment of taxes. If anyone stepped out of line then they would be slapped with the full force of the empire. But behind this show of power and brutality was ultimately a weak man – a player of politics rather than a man of conviction.

When they brought the battered and bruised Man before him, hounded by all kinds of obscure religious bickering and trumped-up charges, Pilate could so easily have asserted his authority as he had on so many other occasions; and yet despite his personal misgivings about the justice of it all, he washed his hands and ducked the responsibility, condemning the Man to a painful criminal's death, knowing him to be innocent. Not the first innocent man to suffer and certainly not the last at the hands of politics and petty rivalry.

When we are confronted by injustice or unfairness, do we stand up for what is right or do we go along with the crowd? Do we speak up for those less fortunate than ourselves or do we perpetuate the stigma and abuse. Do we swagger around our school or workplace with false confidence while inside are terrified of what the cool kids will think of us?

Pause for a moment and think of when you have been weak like Pilate. Ask God to support you when you next have to decide between what is right and what is easy.

Stand up. Be counted.

Our Father …

Second Station: Jesus takes up his cross

There are crosses all around: on lovely bits of jewellery or glorious processional crosses, around the necks of celebrities or on the walls of the homes of believers. Wearing a cross is a powerful witness to the world, not as fashion but as faith: a symbol of victory rather than defeat at the hands of evildoers.

In some ways we have denuded the cross of its power, for what is now a fashion accessory has lost the terror it evokes as an eight-foot-high killing machine: a shocking way to die in pain and humiliation. Crucifixion was not a rare punishment: it was meted out to thousands for everything from pathetic little thefts right up to murder or terrorism. Even grumbling about the occupation by the Romans might end up with you being nailed to your death. Eventually, several hundred years after this sorry event, the Romans would decide that it was even too cruel for them and would ban it.

One of the greatest humiliations was to be forced to carry the instrument of your execution through the streets to the place of your death: a shameful parade for the entertainment of the public – a bit like reality TV these days – not a token or a symbol, but a massive six feet of rough, splintered, heavy wood.

In our lives there are often difficult things that we have to carry with us: worries or anxieties, cares or health problems, difficulties or stressful situations. We often speak of them as being 'crosses we have to bear'. Christ accepted his cross, given him by the world, and willingly took on the burden of this wood, as well as the burden of all the wrong in the world. In taking his cross, he shares your burdens as well. He walks with you, as you walk this journey with him.

Lamb of God …

Third Station: Jesus falls for the first time

He had been arrested late at night, beaten and dragged through the legal system, flogged to within an inch of his life, and forced to carry this heavy burden. Is it any wonder that the Man stumbled to his knees?

These burdens we carry often make us feel that we are stumbling, that we cannot go on. Do we give up and walk away? At the first sign of difficulty in our relationships or families do we break them apart, throw them away? When confronted by a difficult task at work or at school, do we throw our hands into the air and cry, 'I can't do it!'?

So often people (both young people and adults) throw their faith away at the first hint of difficulty. Faith does not promise you a bed of roses and living happily ever after. It does not promise untold riches or ever-lasting happiness because … life happens. Faith promises to support you through all those times: the great times and the not-so-great. Tempting as it might be to throw it all away as soon as life becomes challenging, do not give up on God, because he *never* gives up on you.

Christ had no option but to pick himself up and carry on the enormous task he knew he had to undertake. No going back. No crying off. He continued. And so should you.

Glory be …

Fourth Station: Jesus meets Mary, his Blessed Mother

The story didn't write this down, but the tradition of the Church records it, as does the place in Jerusalem itself: as the Man staggers through the streets, forced to carry his deadly burden, turning the corner, he comes face to face with his mother, Mary. He looks into the eyes of the one who bore him, who loved and nurtured him from his first stirrings in the womb  at the message of an angel through birth and childhood; to adulthood and to this point. The pain of seeing her distress is further torment for him.

The old man in the Temple all those years ago said a sword would pierce her soul. It must have felt like a knife seeing him like this, ripping her apart.

There are those who love us in this world, who care for us and nurture us, whom we often hurt and bring to grief and sadness: through our actions, through our selfishness, through our thoughtlessness. Let us for a moment reflect on those times when we have hurt or upset those who love us and resolve to make amends.

Hail Mary …

Fifth Station: Simon of Cyrene helps Jesus carry his cross

Beaten, flogged, already exhausted and almost at death's door, it appeared that the Man might not survive to his own death. The Romans would have been cruelly punished themselves if that had happened, and so as he almost stumbled again, the soldiers looked around the crowd and picked out Simon, forced him at a sword's point to help the Man, sharing his burden.

Why pick on Simon? The story tells us he came from the town of Cyrene, a place in what is now modern Libya, North Africa. He was in Jerusalem on business. I suppose that his skin colour would have made him stand out in the crowd, and so the Romans picked on him. Because he was different.

So often we ourselves pick on others because of their differences: because they are cleverer or maybe slower than the rest of the class; because they have a different colour skin or come from a different part of God's world; because they have ginger hair or glasses, a different income, education or the wrong kind of trainers or … well, you know why others get picked on, you know why others might seek to bully you.

Because he was picked on, Simon became special: to be remembered and commemorated for ever while the bullies faded into obscurity. He helped shoulder the burdens of another, to help while others turned their backs or ran away in fear.

The next time someone is bullied in your presence, will you be one of the bullies, or one who stands up against the crowd and helps someone carry their burden?

Our Father …

Sixth Station: Jesus meets Veronica

This episode wasn't written about by the four main retellers of the Man's wonderful story, but it doesn't make it any less real. From out of the baying crowd, jeering and spitting at the poor unfortunates trudging to their deaths, steps an old woman. She knows who he is, and as he looks at her, there is a flicker of recognition as he sees her face. A few years back, she was sorely ill, bleeding to death, a weak outcast from society. She reached out to Jesus to be healed, and as she came into contact with the tassle on his prayer shawl, she was healed, in faith.

There is nothing she can do today to repay that, but she needs to do *something*. She unwraps her veil and offers it to the bleeding, sweating man who presses it to his face: a moment's relief on this Friday of torture. He hands it back and smiles in gratitude – their eyes lingering on each other in mutual care and grati-

tude before he is pushed on his way again by the snarling soldier.

After he has gone, Veronica (for that is the name we give her) looks at the veil: on it is imprinted his face, as clear as anything. Blood and sweat have left her with his likeness, and although that may fade, the memory of this moment will never fade.

On one level, this was a trivial gesture, a moment of relief; and yet to him, it meant so much. There is so much unhappiness in this world, so many people wrapped up in their own pain and torment, their insecurities and sadness, that offering them a smile, a comforting word, a hug or a hand can make a small but important difference.

It took bravery to stand out and do something good (however small) for someone. Will you be brave enough?

Lamb of God …

Seventh Station: Jesus falls for the second time

He falls again. This time more severely. Even with help, he is getting weaker and this fall seems to emphasize the pain he feels.

When we mess up, it's often not just once, it's over and over again. Do we give up?

Or do we persevere? Christ had no option. He was forced back up, forced to carry your burden of sin. Shoulder your mistakes with him, and continue your journey of life.

Glory be …

Eighth Station: Jesus encounters the women of Jerusalem

A group of women see him on his fateful journey and begin wailing as is the custom of the time: wailing not necessarily because of their own sadness, but because that is the behaviour which is to be expected.

He stops before them, and tells them not to weep for him, but for themselves and their children. He knows that their conformity to social niceties will not soften the task before him, and perhaps he knows something of what will happen in time, the sadnesses which will befall the children of Israel, the children of the world, from the destruction of Jerusalem and the Temple in AD 70 to the Holocaust of the Second World War.

So much sadness in the world, inflicted on people by people. Through it all, God weeps with them.

At this stage you may not know much about the Holocaust, or the pogroms, or the genocides in Rwanda or Yugoslavia. As you become more aware of the world, you should know of them, for without knowing of these terrible things, you will not be able to prevent the next tragedy: you, the young people of this generation, have the power to prevent such terrible things happening in the future.

Where is God in all this tragedy? With all those who suffer, that's where. In the middle. Suffering with them.[54]

Our Father …

---

54 The most powerful illustration of this comes not from a Christian writer but a Jew, Elie Wiesel, the Holocaust survivor and Nobel prize winner, who described his experience of Auschwitz in a famous book called *Night*. In the face of so much horror and evil many lost their faith; yet for a few it became, paradoxically, a new realization of God's closeness to them. In one harrowing passage Wiesel tells how a young boy was punished by the guards for stealing food. He was hanged on piano wire, while all the other prisoners were forced to watch: 'For more than half an hour the boy stayed there, struggling between life and death, dying in slow agony before our eyes. We were all forced to pass in front of him, but not allowed to look down or avert our eyes, on pain of being hanged ourselves. When I passed in front of him, the child's tongue was still red, his eyes not yet glazed. Behind me a man muttered, "Where is your God now?" And I heard a voice within me answer him, "Where is he? Here he is. He is hanging here on this gallows."'

Ninth Station: Jesus falls for the third time

He falls for the third time. Completely exhausted now, he falls flat on his face. The crowd groan in shock at his condition: the pain of his fall and his humiliation. He can't go on. He *must* go on. This undertaking cannot be avoided. His life's work is at hand.

How do you feel when you fail? It's hard isn't it? You can't run away from life, or difficulties, or upset or pain or hurt. In life, you can't take your ball home in tears. You have to pick yourself up as he did …

Glory be …

Tenth Station: Jesus is stripped of his clothes

When you see those paintings of the crucifixion, he is often portrayed on the cross wearing a little loincloth or a towel around his waist. The Romans weren't that kind. That is there in the paintings to save *your* embarrassment. In reality, you were crucified completely naked. All of you on show in one final humiliation. His clothes are removed from him, and divided up. For the last gar-

ment, they throw dice to see who wins it: further shame.

So often we hide behind our clothes, our attitudes. It's almost like they are shields or masks from which we can be safe from the world. With him there is no need for masks, no recourse to shame or self-pity or insecurity, For he has borne that insecurity for you. Naked, on the cross.

Our Father …

Eleventh Station: Jesus is nailed to the cross

Can you imagine how big the nails have to be in order to pin a grown man to the cross? Longer than the span of an adult's hand. They don't go through the palms, as you so often see in pictures, as that is too weak an area to support the body weight.

The Romans knew just where to put them: through the wrist. They nailed the Man to the heavy crosspiece he had carried through the streets, and then secured that to the vertical part of the cross. Nailing his feet in place before raising it up and slotting it in a hole in the ground.

As the soldiers nailed him in place, he did not cry out curses upon them. He did not throw insults or scream for revenge. He prayed that the Father might forgive them for what they were doing.

The hand on the hammer might have been a Roman one, but each bang of that hammer on the nail that secured him there was from *our* hand. Each lie, each bad word, each tease, each pinch, each punch, each little sin adds to the nail. He took that, for you. And he asks the Father to forgive you.

Lamb of God …

Twelfth Station: Jesus dies on the cross

[Safety warning: I would use this section very sensitively and only with those whom you know well.]

Of course, nailing someone to a cross does not kill them. Crucifixion is far crueller than that. Doctors understand that the act of being suspended by your arms means that your body weight is on your chest, and you cannot breathe.[55] Choking to death, unable to take in a breath, feeling like you are drowning, the panic starts to rise and so you push up on your feet to release the terrible pressure … and the pain in your

---

55 W. D. Edwards et al., 'On the Physical Death of Jesus Christ', *Journal of the American Medical Association*, 1986, http://www.slublog.com/deathjesus.pdf. Accessed December 2012.

chest transfers to the agony in your feet. You take a gasp of air, but the pain in your feet is too much and you buckle, transferring the weight back onto your chest and being unable to breathe: a see-saw of agony, pain and panic as the cycle of pain and asphyxiation repeats again.

I have at times encouraged older teenagers to adopt the 'stress position' with arms outstretched as though on a cross. It's difficult for anyone to do for more than a minute, especially when a 'Roman soldier' is barking at you to keep your hands up. It's very vivid, but not for the timid. You might be better telling them about it and encouraging them to do it themselves, imagining the soldier.

[*Safety warning ends.*]

Three hours. Three hours he hung on the cross. Unimaginable pain.

At the end, he recalls the words of Psalm 22, which begins 'My God, my God, why have you forsaken me?' That psalm may indeed begin as a cry for help, but God on the cross is not God separate from the God in heaven. When you called out the beginning of a psalm, at home, in prayer or in the synagogue, those who heard it would know the whole psalm. Although Psalm 22 begins in torment and separation, the writer recalls God and his saving acts, and it finishes in celebration and triumph. His words do not end in defeat, but in victory.

'It is finished' – he cries, not *I am finished*, but IT is finished – it is complete, it is sorted, it is cancelled: the same phrase written on an IOU or debt record when it gets paid off. Our debt: wiped out. Our sin: defeated.

It is sorted. It is victory.

Our Father …

Glory be …

Thirteenth Station: Jesus is taken down from the cross

If the Romans had just let him faint and allowed him to live, then the team overseeing the execution would have been sentenced to crucifixion themselves: a good incentive to make sure you had done your job properly, I am sure you will agree.

To speed up the other two criminals executed with Jesus, they break their legs. They can no longer push up, and death comes as a merciful release to them. Seeing that Jesus is already dead, they take a spear and thrust it into his side. The witnesses who saw this said that 'blood and water' flowed from the wound, and it showed he was dead.

At the time they didn't know any more than that. It was 2,000 years ago and medical science was very basic. These days, doctors[56] tell us that when a person has been crucified, the pressure in the chest which makes it impossible to breathe builds up fluid around the heart. If a spear went into his heart, blood and this clear, watery fluid would come out. All those years ago they wouldn't know what it was. Even if he were not dead before, this would clearly kill him.

This is one of the ways we know he was truly dead because they described what they saw 2,000 years before we understood scientifically what it meant. It wasn't a faint, it wasn't a fake. It was real death. They took him down and placed him in the arms of his mother for her to cradle as she did when he was a small, hurt child.

All around the world today, mothers in torment cradle their killed, sick or wounded children to them. Others among us suffer from all kinds of illnesses: mental and physical. Pause for a moment and pray for them, for their healing and for the comfort of all those who worry about them.

Hail Mary ...

---

56 W. D. Edwards et al., 'On the Physical Death of Jesus Christ'.

Fourteenth Station: Jesus is laid in the tomb

It is getting dark and the body must be dealt with before sundown and the day of the Sabbath, a holy day in which no work like burying a body may take place. He is taken to a nearby tomb donated by a member of the faithful and he is wrapped in a cloth and placed in the tomb. A huge, heavy stone is placed over it. A Roman guard is tasked to make sure there will be no grave robbery.

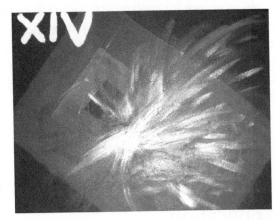

God, all-powerful, all-encompassing, could have burst from the tomb immediately, could have made a big show of what was to come next to leave everyone in no doubt. But God is more subtle than that: we have to wait. Patiently.

We always want things immediately: on-demand movies, instant lotteries, immediate satisfaction. But sometimes we have to wait. Things have to come to fruition.

Like a cocoon, a place of transformation, changes will occur, but in the dark quiet; when we least expect it.

We know that this isn't the end of our story …

Glory be …

Fifteenth Station: Jesus rises from the tomb

I don't believe you can do the stations without the final and most important station: the resurrection. In a church I return back to the altar and have the young people stand right around it.

The story didn't end in the tomb.

On the third day, on the Sunday, very early in the morning, the women came back to the tomb. After a whole Saturday of numbness and grief, they came to complete the burial rites: to anoint the body and rewrap it.

As they get there, the tomb is open! The body is gone! The guards have no idea what has happened: the shroud is not torn away and discarded, but lies as though the body had come back to life!

There are all sorts of ways we know that Jesus beat sin and duffed up death by rising to life again, but for me the best reason is why I have told you this story and led you through these Stations of the Cross. If he hadn't, I wouldn't be wanting to tell you all this, because the living Christ who came back to life and lives today on this very altar, brought here in bread and wine and in the love of his Church, lives in our hearts today: loving, laughing and living on – truly risen! To God be the glory …

Glory be …

Amen.

Application

The theology of the cross is complex and multilayered, and like all good things in the Church it is a profound mystery. No single doctrine can encapsulate it. For me, the idea that Jesus was punished by God for us is a difficult and dangerous perspective; separating the persons of the Trinity and demanding an act of separation between them which is simply not possible. It reduces the figure of God the Father to a bloodthirsty tyrant who must be appeased rather than a loving God who forgives and exercises ultimate power over everything, including sin and death.

Christ did die on the cross for our sins, because it was our sin which put him there. It was our punishment, not God's. God suffered, and God overcame it in the power of the resurrection. This is why the ultimate point of the cross is not punishment, but victory. There is nothing in this world which Christ does not exercise power over, because of the victory of the cross. There is nothing you need fear, because of Christ. For that, you should be truly thankful. You are free. It is sorted.

Resurrection: Ta daa!

Matthew 28.1–8; Mark 16.1–7; Luke 24.1–8; John 20.1–18.

Introduction

The excessive focus by many on the cross risks undermining the point of the cross: the resurrection. Here is God in action. Here is the Messiah vindicated. Here is sin and death defeated. In the agonizingly lost day between Good Friday and Easter Morning, the Orthodox Church does not leave Christ inert. The 'Harrowing of Hell' sees Christ entering the very gates of evil, destroying them in the process, and rescuing the inhabitants therein. This is why the tombs burst open on Easter morning[57] and why, even while many might cling to a visceral vision of hell, and the Church accepts the existence of a place where God may be absent,[58] there is no one there …

Preparation

You will need eggs for this activity. They can be hard-boiled or (better) blown. The instructions for preparing the eggs are listed below. You will also need paint, food dye or felt-tip pens, stickers, glitter and other decorative items appropriate to the age of the young people you are working with. However, never underestimate the simple joy a group of teenagers can derive from a little bit of childish 'cutting and sticking'.

Story

'Guard this tomb,' they said.
   'This tomb?' says I.
   'No, that tomb …' 'That tomb?' 'Yes.' 'The new one?' 'Yes.'

---

57 Matthew 27.52.
58 Church of England Doctrine Commission, *The Mystery of Salvation*, Church House Publishing, 1995, p. 199.

I like orders when they are simple. No complications.

It wasn't going to be a hard job, was it? Guard a tomb! At least them inside aren't going to want to try and escape …

We were detailed to the tomb just as they were putting the body inside. It was getting dark, so these Jews were in a bit of a hurry. It looked like the bloke had been nailed to one of them crosses: a nasty brutish, horrible way to die. I never liked doing them crucifixions: if you mess it up and the criminal gets off the cross, or someone rescues them or anything else that means they end up by not dying, then they crucify you … really … they have you nailed up there, so the incentive is right to make sure they are dead – proper dead. We used to break their legs, which killed them a bit quicker – an act of mercy in the midst of a cruel torture. If they were already dead, then a quick spear in the side makes doubly sure they're dead and so you won't be next. Ugh, makes me shudder just to think about what we have to do to them. I see this one must have died quickish, as amid the bruises and bleeding there was this big wound in his side: a bit of blood and the clear fluid that looks like water dripping out from it, I know that only happens when you die.

Then they seal the tomb with this really big rock. Took about a dozen men to lever it into place. It keeps the tomb secure and free from grave-robbers. I dunno why we have to guard it: I saw he wasn't going to try and get out; I suppose it's to prevent anyone nicking the body – though what they'd do with it beats me … I mean they couldn't put strings on it and pretend he was alive or anything …

All Saturday we stood guard. A few people, mainly women, came to the tomb in tears; proper lost they looked, real sad. I could tell a lot of his followers had stayed away. Maybe they thought it wasn't such a good time to be seen as another trouble-maker like he clearly was … and end up with the same fate.

Then on the Sunday, really early like, just as the sun is rising, something really weird happens. One minute I'm guarding the tomb with everything as it should be and the next it's like the place has exploded in light. It's so strong that I'm knocked off my feet.

By the time I've pulled myself up and sorted out my helmet which had fallen over my eyes, I can see that the huge great stone has been moved, and although that light isn't there any more, it's not totally dark, like there is something dancing on the breeze, and there is a small but clear difference in the wind, on the air: like sparkles of glitter, like … angels dancing in the air.

Me and the squad have just turned and run for the trees: a tactical retreat is what I plan to say in the report. I can still see all that's going on and if any of those rebels we were warned about try and come to take the body and hide it, we're ready – a bit scared, but ready. But instead of an attacking army, or even a squad of rebels, it's just a bunch of women. They see the open tomb and look terrified. Some of them rush off immediately but one of them – what was the name I overhead? Mary? She stays, and sits weeping.

This bloke comes up slowly behind her, I suppose it must have been one of the garden staff, and says something to her. She's crying about the missing body and all that … wait a minute – I didn't see anyone take the body – no one's been in that tomb since we found it open. He says something else to her, which I didn't quite get 'cause these locals don't half talk funny, but she turns to face him and falls to her feet in front of him and instead of crying, she's all happy … I don't get women at the best of times but this …

Off she trots and the gardener bloke … well, he's just not there any more.

The women must have told someone because two guys come running quick as you can. The younger one was a bit quicker and he skids to a halt at the entrance. The big burly one – looked an active type, a fisherman maybe – he goes straight in and in a moment is out again. Just him. He has in his hand a cloth which looks like it was wrapped around the head. He is muttering something about angels and looking for the living among the dead. He's back in and grabs the burial shroud and off they go like something amazing has happened.

I know no one has come out with the body, so I ventures out from the tree cover to approach the entrance. I peek inside (a bit nervous like) and see … nothing.

An empty tomb. No body. Geddit? No. Body. Nobody!

Well, I put in my report that I never saw no one take any body – I mean, they'd have me on a charge, have me nailed to a cross for letting the body get stolen. I'm sticking by the truth, no matter how strange it sounds.

I'm sure they'll come up with all kinds of explanations, but all I know is there was a dead body, there isn't one now and I certainly didn't see it getting nicked.

I didn't see any more of the gardener, either. Funny that …

Activity: Egg painting

Many cultures across the world and especially in Eastern Europe paint eggs as part of their Easter celebrations.

Although this is often done at Eastertime, it might be useful to do this outside the Easter season and emphasize that the Easter story isn't just a once-a-year event, but a daily celebration of the new life found in Christ.

However, raw eggs aren't good for this task: they break and they go off quickly. You need to de-egg your shells before you start making them beauti-

ful. You can hard-boil them, or you can blow them. If you really want your eggs to last, you should blow them, as hard-boiled eggs do go bad within a few weeks.

For the very young, hard-boiling is probably best, as blown eggs can be fragile and this would make them more suited for teenagers.

How to Blow Eggs

Equipment:

- Egg
- Large needle, such as for darning or upholstering
- Skewer
- Bowl

Take your egg in one hand, and a large darning-needle in the other. Then make a small hole in one end with the needle, trying not to crack the shell around the hole.

It's best to scratch the point where you intend to make your hole gradually, rather than go in with force. Don't put the egg down on the table to make the hole, as it will break.

Make another hole at the other end of the egg, and widen both holes a little, carefully. The one at the bottom should be a little larger than the one on top.

Then break the contents of the egg up to make it easier to get it out. Push a skewer in through one of your holes, and pierce the yoke.

Place a bowl under your egg and, taking a deep breath, blow at a consistent rate through the hole in the top. The contents of the egg gradually come out through the bottom hole, ready to be scrambled for supper later: a special bonus!

Once the egg is empty, fill it with cold water, swish the water around, and let it out of the bottom hole. Do this two or three times to clean the inside. Don't use hot water, as this might bake some of the egg white on to the inside of the shell.

Put your egg in a pre-heated oven, Gas Mark 1 (300°F/150°C), for 10–15 minutes. This both dries it out and prepares it to be painted.

Painting an Egg

Using paint brushes and paints, food colouring or felt-tip pens, you can go to town with the decorations. Young children can finger-paint or create wild abstract colourful creations, whereas teenagers, and those with more artistic ambitions, will benefit from fine paintbrushes. These don't need to be expensive, and really add to the detail you can put on an egg.

Eggs can be figurative, or abstract: the only limit is your imagination!

You can also add to your eggs by using stickers, glue and glitter, cut-out shapes (cut out yourself, or bought ready-made) or stencils. These can be used in conjunction with dyes and paints, or on their own.

After all that, enjoy your beautiful Easter eggs!

Application

The whole of the Christian faith hinges upon the resurrection. The point of the cross was not punishment, but in order for Christ to deliver victory over sin and death. The empty tomb is the proof of that.

That Christ died on the cross is incontrovertible, that he was unable to be rescued from the cross in life, nor stolen from the tomb in death is clear because the penalties on those charged with the task were to ensure that their tasks were fulfilled.

The resurrection happens in secret, seen only by God and his holy messengers, but the aftermath of it ultimately affects the whole world. If you were going to fake the resurrection, steal the body and claim he was risen from the dead, you wouldn't do it like this:

- The first witnesses you would choose for credibility would not be women. Society and culture back then had an even less egalitarian sense than now and a woman's testimony was inadmissible in a court of law and was therefore worthless.[59]
- Christ appeared to so many people that it couldn't have been either a secret conspiracy kept between a handful of people or a mass hallucination. Hallucinations don't sit down and eat food with you, breathe on you and bless you or hold conversations with you.
- Last and most importantly: if this whole thing was a fake, then surely at the first opportunity the co-conspirators had to recant rather than be martyred, and they would have admitted it was a lie. All of the apostles and countless others went to their own deaths proclaiming 'We have seen the risen Lord' and you cannot fake that.

---

59 I apologize for this, but that's how it was.

Conclusion

This book ends with the resurrection, because it is the beginning for us. I pray that it may have inspired you to reach out to young people with the stories that inspire you. Not all the key stories could be included here from either the Holy Scriptures or the life and witness of the Church. It is now up to you and your young people to fill in the gaps!

May God bless you richly as you walk on in his way. Amen.

References

M. Anderson and P. Heesome, *What a Day: Stations of the Cross for Young People*, Kevin Mayhew, 1998.

Church of England Doctrine Commission, *The Mystery of Salvation*, Church House Publishing, 1995.

V. Donovan, *Christianity Rediscovered*, SCM Press, 2001.

L. Pierson, *Storytelling: A Practical Guide*, Scripture Union, 1997.

Elie Wiesel, *Night*, Bantam Books, 1960.